Presented to

Erin

from Tot's Group

The Vine Community Church

Littleport July 2021.

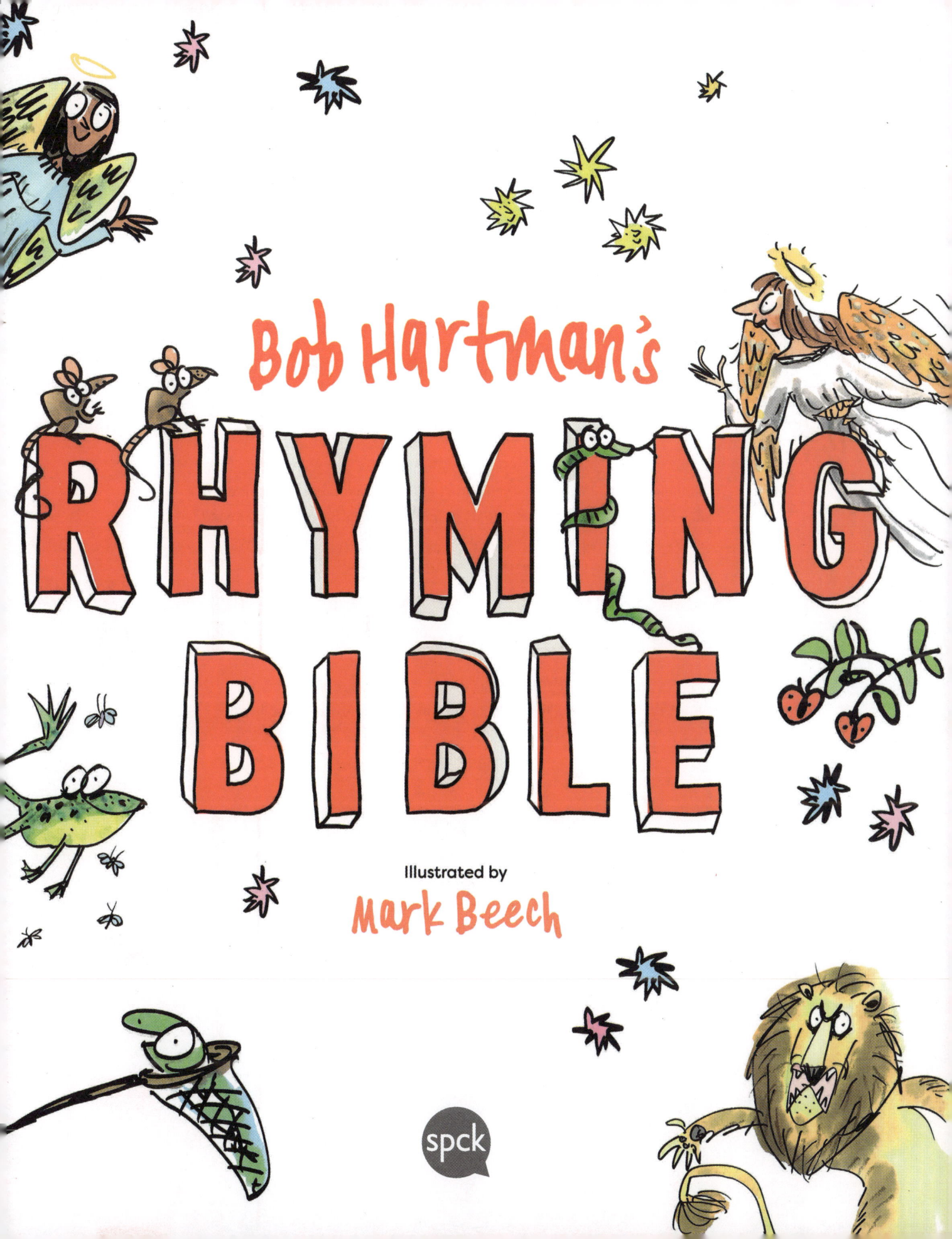

Bob Hartman's RHYMING BIBLE

Illustrated by
Mark Beech

spck

First published in Great Britain in 2019

Society for Promoting Christian Knowledge
36 Causton Street
London SW1P 4ST
www.spck.org.uk

Text copyright © Bob Hartman 2019
Illustrations copyright © Mark Beech 2019

All rights reserved. No part of this book may be reproduced or transmitted in any form or by any means, electronic or mechanical, including photocopying, recording, or by any information storage and retrieval system, without permission in writing from the publisher.

SPCK does not necessarily endorse the individual views contained in its publications.

British Library Cataloguing-in-Publication Data
A catalogue record for this book is available from the British Library

ISBN 978–0–281–07794–6
1 3 5 7 9 10 8 6 4 2

Designed by Mandy Norman
First printed in Turkey by Mega Print
Subsequently digitally printed in Great Britain

Produced on paper from sustainable forests

CONTENTS

OLD TESTAMENT STORIES

It's all good!
Creation – Genesis 1.1—2.3 — 2

A snake in the grass
The fall – Genesis 3 — 4

A floating zoo
Noah and the ark – Genesis 6.1—9.17 — 7

A really tall tower
The Tower of Babel – Genesis 11.1–9 — 10

A child called Laughter
Abram and Sarai – Genesis 12.1–5; 18.1–15; 21.1–7 — 13

God will provide
Abraham and Isaac – Genesis 22 — 15

Hairy and tricksy
Jacob and Esau – Genesis 25.19–34, 27 — 17

Coats and dreams
Joseph part 1 – Genesis 37   **20**

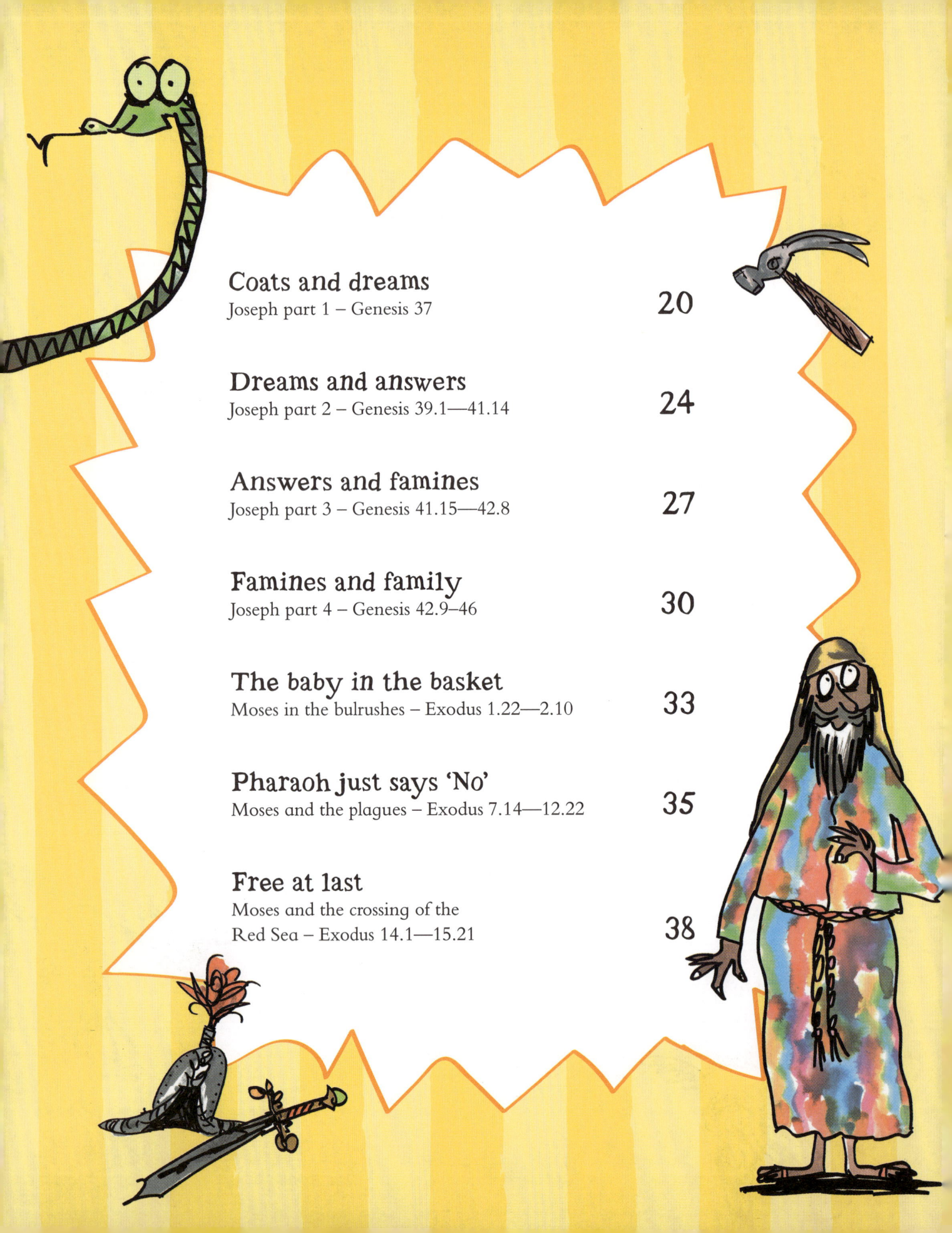

Dreams and answers
Joseph part 2 – Genesis 39.1—41.14   **24**

Answers and famines
Joseph part 3 – Genesis 41.15—42.8   **27**

Famines and family
Joseph part 4 – Genesis 42.9–46   **30**

The baby in the basket
Moses in the bulrushes – Exodus 1.22—2.10   **33**

Pharaoh just says 'No'
Moses and the plagues – Exodus 7.14—12.22   **35**

Free at last
Moses and the crossing of the
Red Sea – Exodus 14.1—15.21   **38**

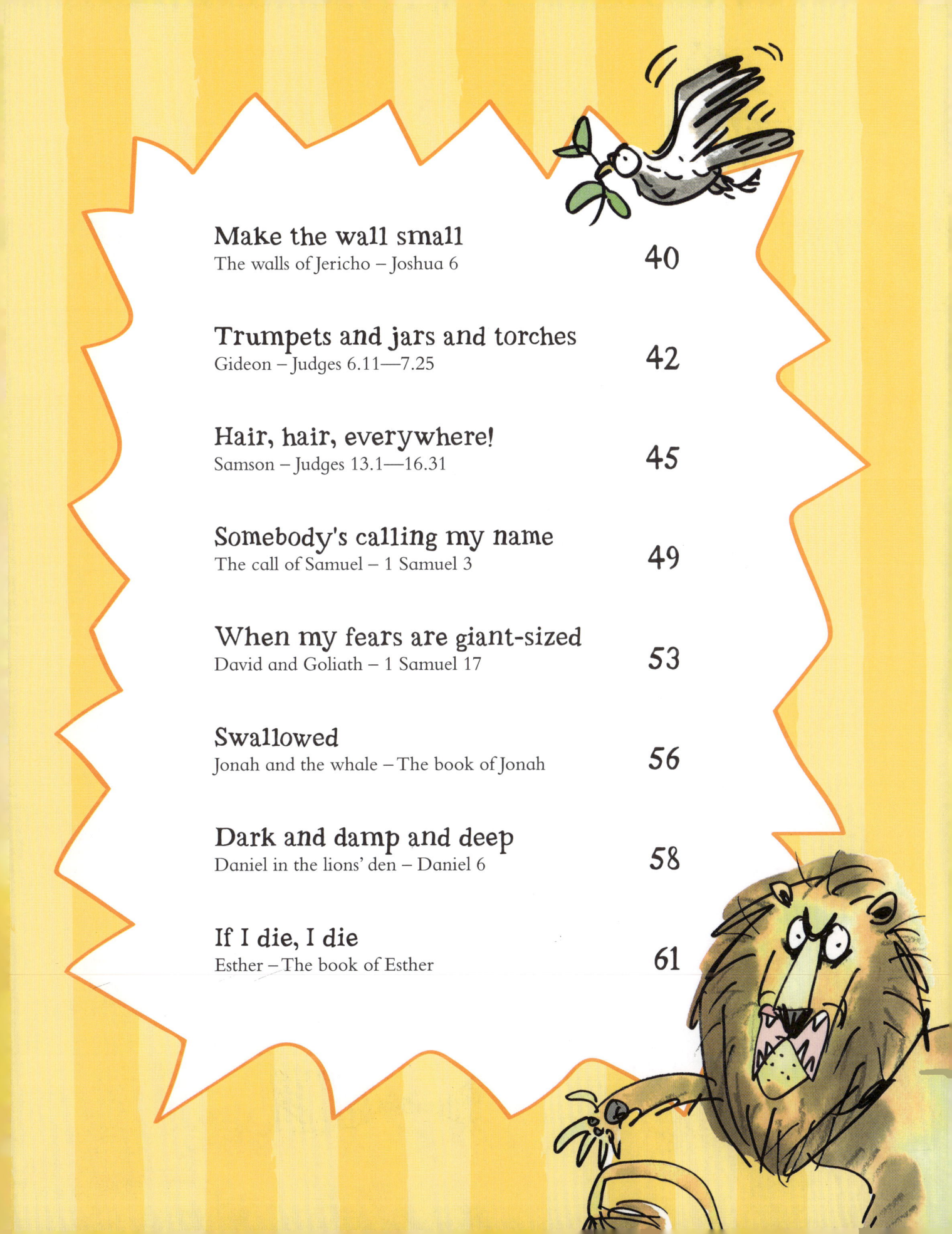

Make the wall small
The walls of Jericho – Joshua 6 — 40

Trumpets and jars and torches
Gideon – Judges 6.11—7.25 — 42

Hair, hair, everywhere!
Samson – Judges 13.1—16.31 — 45

Somebody's calling my name
The call of Samuel – 1 Samuel 3 — 49

When my fears are giant-sized
David and Goliath – 1 Samuel 17 — 53

Swallowed
Jonah and the whale – The book of Jonah — 56

Dark and damp and deep
Daniel in the lions' den – Daniel 6 — 58

If I die, I die
Esther – The book of Esther — 61

NEW TESTAMENT STORIES

A woman called Mary
The Annunciation – Luke 1.26–38
66

Joseph, don't worry
An angel speaks to Joseph – Matthew 1.18–25
70

It begins in Bethlehem
Shepherds hear good news – Luke 2.8–21
72

One hump, two humps
Wise men visit Jesus – Matthew 2.1–12
75

Fill in all the valleys
John the Baptist baptizes Jesus – Luke 3.1–22
78

Come and follow me
The call of the disciples – Matthew 4.18–22
80

One friend, two friends, three friends, four
Jesus heals a paralysed man – Luke 5.17–26
82

Rumbling tummies
The feeding of the five thousand – John 6.1–14
84

Every last son
The prodigal son – Luke 15.11–32
86

Sow, sow, sow your seeds
The parable of the sower – Matthew 13.1–23
90

Every last lamb
The parable of the lost sheep – Luke 15.1–7
94

Waiting in line
Jesus and the children – Mark 10.13–16
96

Little man up in the tree
Jesus meets Zacchaeus – Luke 19.1–10
98

The clip-clop beat
Palm Sunday – Luke 19.28–40
101

Body and blood and bread and wine
The Last Supper – Matthew 26.17–30
104

When Jesus hung upon the cross
The crucifixion – John 19.17–30; Luke 2.26–49
108

No more crying
The empty tomb – John 20.1–18
110

Not a ghost story
Jesus appears to his followers – John 20.19–29; Acts 1.1–11
114

Blowing wind and tongues of flame
Pentecost – Acts 2.1–41
116

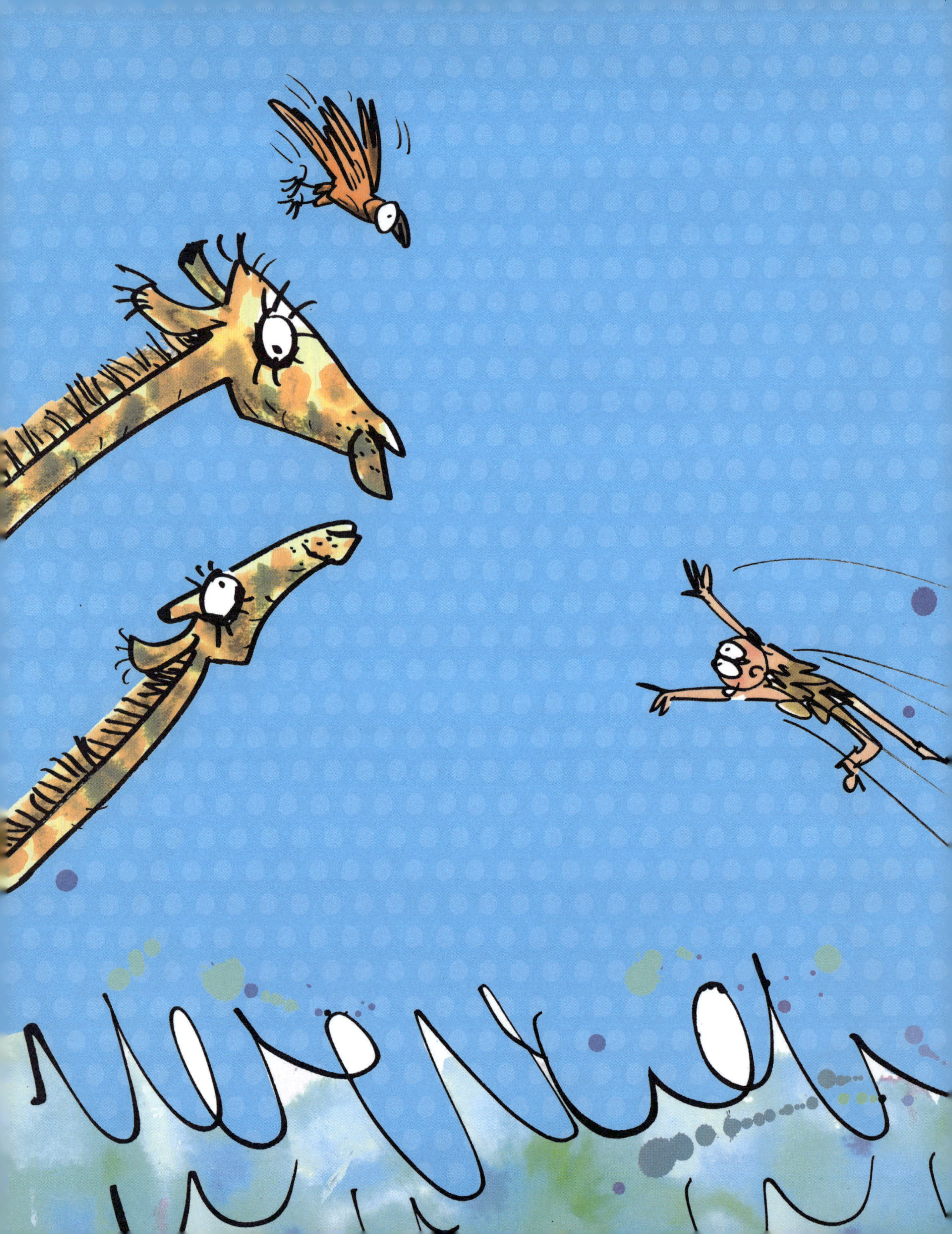

OLD TESTAMENT STORIES

It's ALL good!

There was nothing, at first, there was nothing but **God**.
No planets, no mountains, no chickens, no cod.
Then God said the word, and like that, there was **light**!
The light he called Day and the dark he called Night.

And then God said **'water'**, and water there was,
The waters below, and the waters above.
And just like a canopy, way up on high,
The bright baby blue and the white cloudy sky.

And when God said 'gather', the waters below
Washed into seas with a **tumbling flow**,
And left behind dry land, the dark fertile earth,
Where flowers and trees and fruit came to birth.

God spoke into being the sun, stars and moon,
For morning and evening and night-time and noon.
Light for the darkness and light for the day
To mark off the seasons as years pass away.

'Now fill up the oceans', said God, gurgling, 'Fish!'
And fin, tail and tentacle answered his wish.
And when he cried, 'Bird!', a sky-full replied,
With a **squawk** and swoop and a duck and a dive.

When God **roared** their names, the wild beasts appeared.
'Now, cattle,' said God . 'Now sheep to be sheared.
Now animals big. Now animals small.
Now creatures who slither and skitter and crawl.'

And then, with a smile God said 'Women and Men.
Made in my image, made to be friends.
Made to make babies, sweet boys and girls.
Made to take care of my *beautiful world.*'

And when he had finished, as most artists should,
God looked at his work. And he said, 'It's all GOOD!'
And when he had finished, as most artists do,
He rested, and then blessed that day of rest, too.

A SNAKE in the GRASS

So God said to **Adam** and God said to **Eve**,
'Here's a garden that you can call home.
A beautiful, paradise place called Eden,
Where you can just wander and roam.

'Eat what you like, pluck fruit from each branch,
Except for the **Knowledge Tree**.
For that one will show you both evil and good,
And, sadly, you'll have to leave.'

So Adam and Eve stayed away from that tree,
And did all that God said they should.
They walked and they talked with him every day,
And life was incredibly good.

Then, one day, the serpent stopped by for a chat,
A clever and LYING BEAST.
'Take a bite from the Knowledge Tree's fruit!' he said.
'I hear it makes quite a nice feast.'

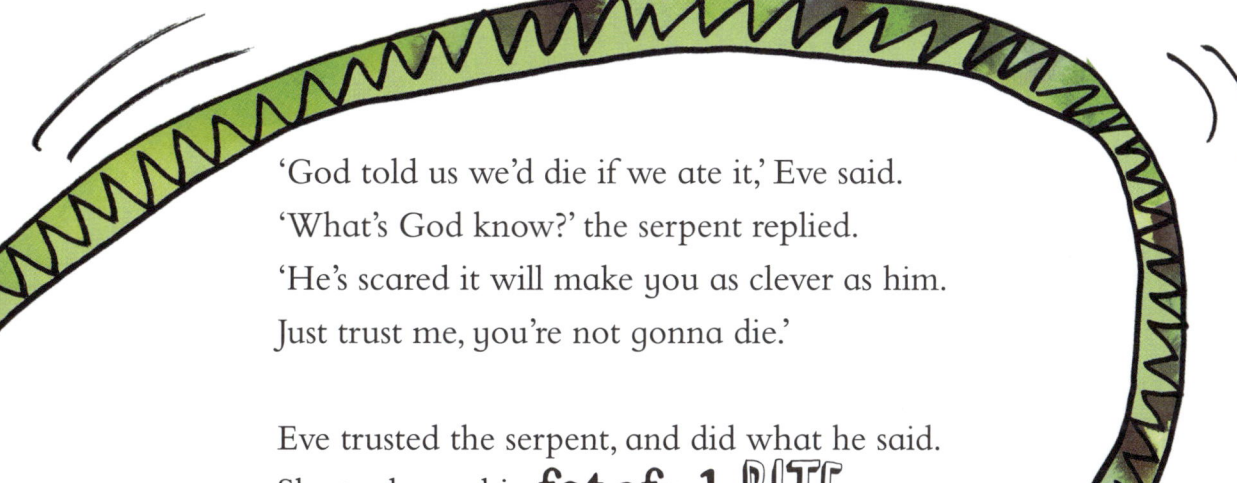

'God told us we'd die if we ate it,' Eve said.
'What's God know?' the serpent replied.
'He's scared it will make you as clever as him.
Just trust me, you're not gonna die.'

Eve trusted the serpent, and did what he said.
She took one big **fateful BITE**.
And Adam did too, and that's when they knew
That things were no longer right.

'You're naked,' Eve cried. 'Yeah, you're naked, too!'
Cried Adam. 'Quick, grab some plants!'
And fashioned from fig leaves, first-fruit of the loom,
A couple of pairs of pants.

When God came to call in the cool of the day,
Eve and Adam **ducked** into the trees.
When God called their names, they **trembled** and said,
'We're hiding, we're naked, you see.'

'Who said you were naked?' God sighed, 'Yes I see.
You've eaten the fruit from that tree.'
'It's her fault!' said Adam, pointing at Eve.
'It's the serpent!' she cried. **'NOT ME!'**

'You each will be punished,' God sadly declared.
'Just fruits of your fruit-eating fall.
The **serpent will crawl**, and one of Eve's seed
Will finish him once and for all.

'Eve will be cursed with **PAIN**, giving birth.
And Adam will crack the earth's crust
With hard sweat and toil, to bring food from soil,
Then die and return to the dust.'

When God had made clothes from animal skins
For Adam and for his wife,
He sent them away and called for an *angel*
To guard the great **Tree of Life**.

For God knows what's best and God knows what's right.
His truth will forever last.
If anyone tells you otherwise,
He lies like that **SNAKE** in the grass.

A floating ZOO

When God looked at all the people he'd made,
He sighed at the sight of them.
'They're really quite bad.
It makes me so sad.
I think I should start again.'

He managed to find just one good man, though.
So God called to **Noah** by name,
'Build a big boat.
Make sure it will float.
I warn you, it's going to **rain!**'

Then Noah did all God told him to do.
He followed God's pattern, true.
He built a great **ARK**
From gopher wood bark,
And the rest of the gopher wood, too.

He warned all his neighbours the rains would come,
But they all just laughed in his face.
'Your boat is a **joke**.
Who cares if it floats?
We never get floods in this place.'

'Now Noah,' God said, 'here's another small job:
I want you to build me a ZOO.
Hippos and hares
   Beavers and bears
      A couple of each will do.'

      So Noah collected a world-full of BEASTS,
        Menageried, two by two.
          Donkeys and dogs,
            Ferrets and frogs,
              Kittens and kangaroos.

      When Noah had loaded the beasts on board,
        And all of his family, too,
          God shut the door.
        It started to pour.
      Just eight members in the crew.

    So Noah, his wife, their three sons and wives,
Were safe, as the waters rose high.
      But down on the ground,
      Everyone drowned,
    As rain fell in sheets from the sky.

For **forty long DAYS**,
    and **forty long nights**,
The rain never ceased to fall.
Water like fountains
Covered the mountains,
No bits of land left, at all.

Floating alone on the **watery world**,
One hundred and fifty days,
Noah just waited.
He hoped and he prayed that
The floods would all go away.

The ark came to rest on Ararat,
A mountaintop stop so tall.
Noah sent from his hand
A bird to find land,
But the raven found nothing at all.

So Noah sent out a white dove instead,
And when it came back with a leaf,
He knew at long last
That the flooding was past
And his passengers all could leave.

So out they all poured, and God told them plain
To claim the whole earth, fresh and new.
'Fill up my world
With boys and with girls
And, yes, baby animals, too.'

Then up in the sky, God painted a sign:
A RAINBOW, a promise above.
'I never will send
Rain like this rain again
And cover the world in a flood.'

A really TALL TOWER

Back in the days
when the world was quite young,
There was only one language.
That's right, **only one**.

No Swedish or English
And no Portuguese.
Just one common tongue
They all spoke with ease.

Not sure what they called it.
We don't know its name.
But everyone used it,
And all spoke the same.

So when they went east
To a place they called *Shinar*,
They decided to make
A city much finer.

And because, when they spoke,
They could all understand,
They concocted together
A really BIG PLAN.

They made **hardened BRICKS**.
Stone was not good enough.
And they **glued** them together
With bitumen stuff.

'Now let's build a **TOWER**,'
They said with one tongue.
'High in the sky,
To impress everyone.

'And a city around it,
Shiny and **new**,
To amaze the whole world
With the things we can do.

'We'll climb up to **heaven**,
Rule over the plain.
And people will always
Remember our name.'

Then God had a look
And he wasn't that pleased.
'They'll do what they want, now.
They'll do it with ease,'

He said with a sigh.
'So here is my plan:
I'll **MIX UP** their language
They won't understand.

'One will speak clearly.
His mate will go **"Huh?"**
Then his friend will explain
And he'll just go **"What?"**

'They'll put down their hammers
And put down their bricks
And wonder why everyone
Else is so thick.'

And that's just what happened.
They couldn't go on.
With their language confused,
Their project was done.

So they **dropped** all their tools,
Left them there on the table,
And wandered away,
And called the place BABEL.

They **scattered** themselves
Far away from the plain.
And with so many tongues
Found it hard to explain

Why, despite all they did
To find fortune and fame,
That nobody, nowhere,
Remembers their name.

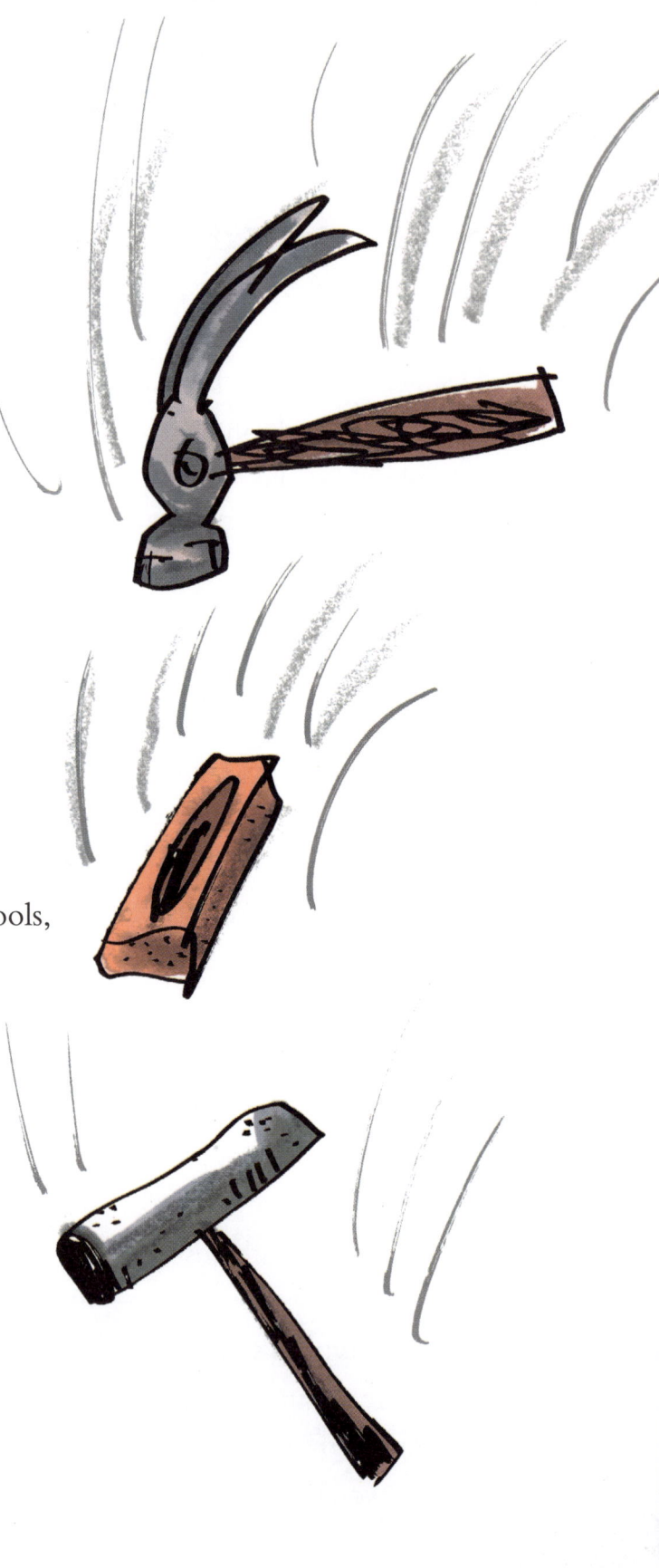

A child called LAUGHTER

So God said to Abram, 'I want you to leave
Your country, your kindred and roam.
Your children will bless every nation on earth.
Follow me to your new home!'

Now Abram was old and his wife, Sarah, too,
Without any children. **NOT ONE!**
But he trusted God's promise and followed his lead,
And went till the journey was done.

Beautiful, prosperous Canaan land
Was the name of his destination.
'But I still have no children,' said Abram to God.
'So how can I start a great nation?'

'Look up in the sky,' God whispered to Abram.
'Count every star that you see.
I'll give you more children than all of those stars,
Even more than the sands in the sea.'

And just to make certain his promise was real,
God even changed Abram's name.
'You're "Abraham", now, which means
Father of Nations.
And, yes, it does sound much the same!'

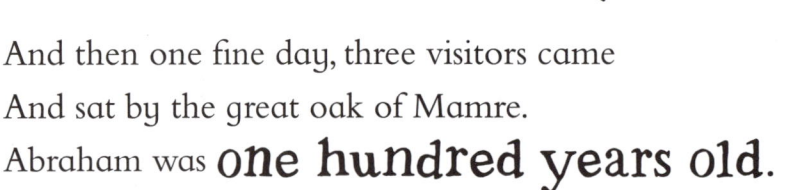

And then one fine day, three visitors came
And sat by the great oak of Mamre.
Abraham was **one hundred years old**.
And Sarah a quite sprightly ninety.

Abraham offered his guests a fine meal,
Then hurried into his tent.
'You bake the cakes, Sarah, I'll cook a calf.
We'll find out why these gents were sent.'

The food was delicious, a proper feast.
'We'll be back in a year,' the guests smiled.
'By then you will have one more mouth to feed:
A baby.
A son. SARAH'S CHILD!'

Alone in the tent, Sarah listened amazed.
She chuckled and then laughed out loud.
'Why is she laughing?' the guests asked, as one.
'We know what we're talking about!'

And so the guests went and, within the year,
As promised, God answered all of their dreams.
Sarah gave birth to a boy they called LAUGHTER
For that's what the name Isaac means!

God will provide

God said to Abraham, here is a test:
'Take Isaac, the son you love,
And **kill** him and **burn** him, an offering to me,
High up in the mountains above.'

So off they both went to the land of Moriah,
Abraham and his loved son,
The old man astride his saddled donkey,
To kill his long-promised one.

And when he had cut enough wood for the fire,
Abraham followed God's lead
To the sacrifice place, three days' journey away,
To do that most **AWFUL DEED**.

And when they'd arrived, he said to his servants,
'Leave us to climb a bit higher.'
Then strapping the wood on to young Isaac's back,
He picked up the knife and the fire.

'Father,' said Isaac, 'the wood's on my back,
And you have the **fire** and the **knife**,
But where is the lamb that we'll burn on the altar,
The lamb that will give up its life?'

'We'll leave that to God,' old Abraham said.
'We'll trust him to do what is right.
He'll give us the lamb for the sacrifice fire.
I know that our **God will provide**.'

But then when the old man had fashioned an altar,
He tied up his promised one,
And laid him, an offering, on top of the wood,
And raised the knife over his son.

'Abraham, STOP!' an angel voice cried.
'Don't harm one hair on your boy's head.
God knows you would give him you own precious son.
Kill that ram in the thicket, instead.'

So Abraham took the ram that was there,
And offered him up to the Lord.
He called that place simply, **'God will provide'**.
And that's when he heard these words:

'Look up in the sky,' God promised, again.
'Count every star that you see.
I'll give you more children than all of those stars,
Even more than the sands in the sea.'

HAIRY and TRICKSY

Rebecca and Isaac's twin baby boys
Were born a few minutes apart.
They didn't have much in common, though.
They were **different** right from the start.

When ESAU came out, he had red bushy hair.
And sweet baby JACOB had none.
But he had his hand on his big brother's heel,
A sign of the problems to come.

Isaac loved Esau, his **BIG HAIRY!** son,
Who brought him the best fresh meat.
But Jacob stayed home and learned tricks from his mum
And turned into quite a good cheat.

So one day, when Esau came home from a hunt,
He found Jacob cooking a meal.
'I'm starving!' he said.
'Give me some of that now!'
Said Jacob, 'I'll do you a deal.

'Our father's inheritance passes to you,
For you are his firstborn child.
Trade me that birthright for this bowl of stew,
And then you can eat,' Jacob smiled.

So Esau agreed, and that bad deed was done.
And Jacob did **happy flips.**

Just one thing remained to seal the whole deal:
A blessing from Isaac's own lips.

As Isaac grew older, his eyesight grew weak.
'Dear Esau,' he said, with a sigh.
'Catch me some game. Make my favourite meal.
I'll bless you before I die.'

Rebecca gave Isaac's instructions to Jacob.
'And here is my plan,' she said.
'Fetch me **TWO GOATS** and we'll cook up that meal,
And you'll get the blessing, instead.'

'My arms are not HAIRY! Father will guess.
The trick will not work!' Jacob cried.
'We'll cover your arms with the skin of the goat,'
Tricksy Rebecca replied.

So into old Isaac's tent Jacob went,
Goat on the plate (and his arms!)
'Here's food for you, father,' Jacob announced.
But Isaac was slightly alarmed.

'The food's come so quickly, Esau my boy.
Your hunt was a great success.
But strangely your voice sounds just like your brother's.
I'd swear it was him, at a guess.

'Now give me your HAND so that I can be sure.'
And the fake arm-hair worked a treat.
He thought it was Esau, and spoke out a blessing,
Which Jacob quite gladly received.

When Esau appeared with a meal, sometime later,
Isaac felt bad for his son.
'I've already given your brother my blessing.
There's nothing that can be done.'

So Esau then VOWED TO MURDER his brother.
And Jacob ran far from home,
Blessed by his father, heir to his name,
But forced for a while to ROAM.

COATS and DREAMS

Joseph dreamed.
　　　　His brothers schemed.
And when it all was through,
God dreamed Joseph's dream with him.
And Joseph's dream came **TRUE**.

Joseph was the **favourite son**
Of Jacob, his old dad.
So Joseph did a lot of things
That made his brothers **MAD**.

He snitched on them, when they did wrong.
That really got their goat.
But what they hated most of all
Was Joseph's **lovely coat**.

Jacob made it many-coloured,
Reds and golds all round.
While all the other brothers had to wear
Were coats of brown … **and brown**.

Then Joseph started having dreams.
'I think this is a sign.
We all had sheaves of wheat,' he said.
'And yours bowed down to **mine!**'

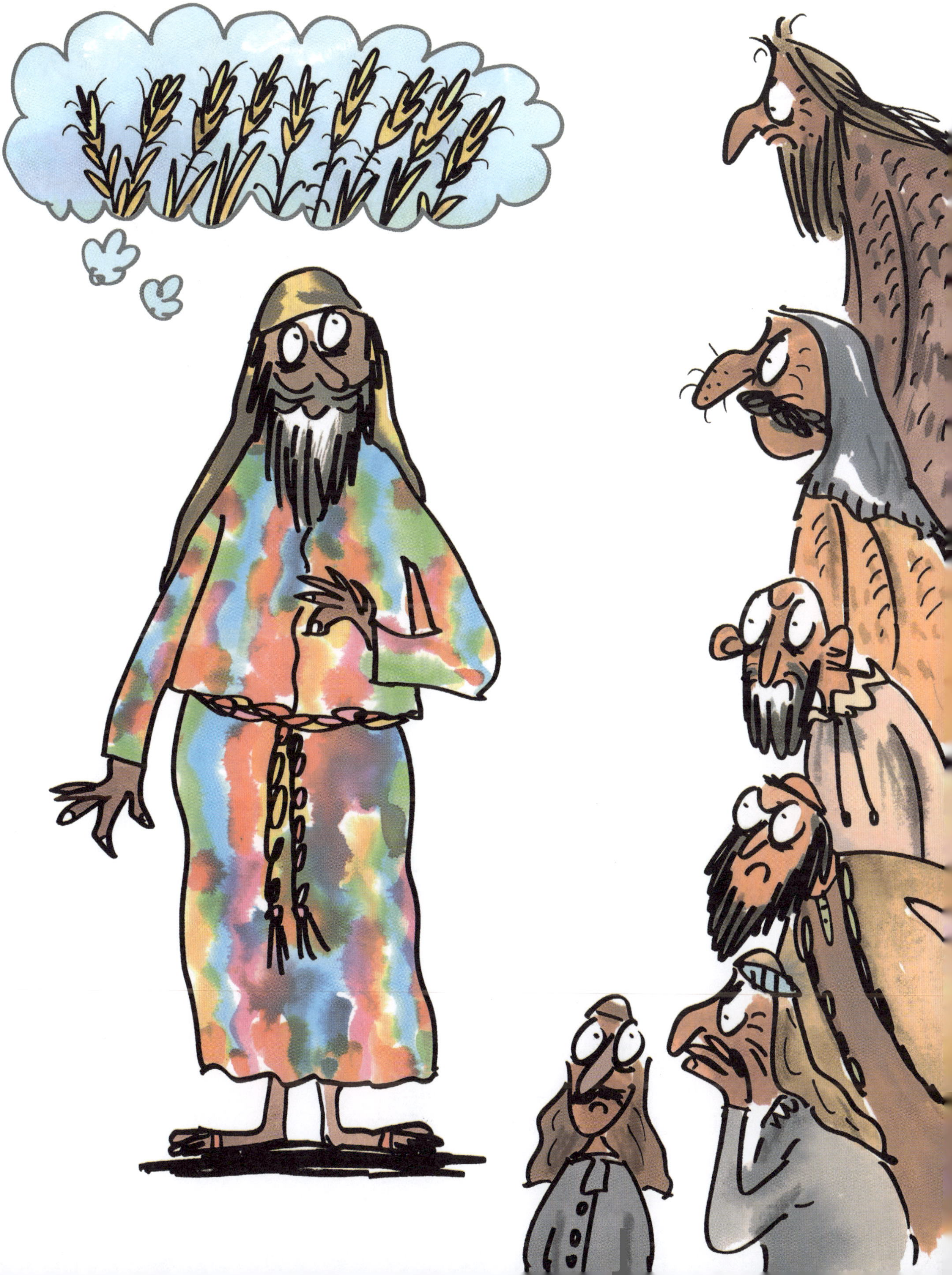

'And then I dreamed that you were **stars**,
And Father was the **sun**.
And you all joined with Mum, the **moon**,
To honour me, as one.'

That really was the final straw.
The brothers were **FED UP**.
The time had come, they all agreed,
To deal with this proud pup.

So when they got him on his own,
Out in the fields one day,
They grabbed him and they made a pact
To take his coat away.

'We'll take his life, as well,' they cried.
'And end this dreamer's dreams.
We'll say a lion ate him up.'
It was an **EVIL SCHEME**.

And then one brother said as much.
REUBEN was his name.
'I will not take my brother's life.
I will not take the blame.

'Let's put him in this pit,' he said.
'Make him **stew** and POUT.'
(He hoped to come back, later on,
And pull his brother out.)

But just as soon as Reuben left,
Some traders wandered by.
'Let's sell the dreamer as a slave,'
Brother Judah cried.

Twenty silver coins they got.
Then they **killed** a goat,
And took its blood and spread it on
The many-coloured coat.

They showed it to poor JACOB
To prove his son had died.
While off to Egypt Joseph went,
A slave all bound and tied.

Joseph dreamed. His brothers SCHEMED.
And when it all was through,
God dreamed Joseph's dream with him.
And Joseph's dream came TRUE.

Dreams and Answers

Joseph dreamed. His brothers SCHEMED.
And when it all was through,
God dreamed Joseph's dream with him.
And Joseph's dream came TRUE.

When Joseph got to Egypt,
They sold him as a **slave**
To Pharaoh's captain, POTIPHAR,
A soldier strong and brave.

'You've served me well,' said Potiphar,
When many months had passed.
'So run my household, Joseph.
And may our friendship last.'

The captain, sadly, had a wife
With eyes for other men.
And, yes, she fancied Joseph
As more than just a friend.

But when she tried to kiss him,
    Quite rightly, he said, 'NO!'

She loudly sighed, and then she cried,
'To Potiphar I'll go.'

'Dear husband,' she lied, weeping
And **wiggling** her hips,
'Joseph came to me and put
His lips upon my lips.'

So off to prison Joseph went,
At Potiphar's request.
And there he met a **cupbearer**,
A BAKER and the rest.

The baker and the cupbearer
Dreamed some puzzling dreams.
'Tell me, please,' said Joseph.
'God will show me what they mean.'

'In **MY** dream,' said the **cupbearer**,
'Three branches sprouted grapes.
I squeezed them into Pharaoh's cup.
Could that mean I escape?'

'It could!' said Joseph, smiling.
'In only three days' time,
You'll serve again in Pharaoh's house,
And all will be just fine.'

'In **MY** dream,' said the BAKER,
'Three basketfuls of bread,
Were eaten by a bunch of birds
Right there from my head.'

'Oh dear,' said Joseph, sadly.
'In only three days' time,
You'll lose your head, and on your flesh
The hungry birds will dine.'

Both dreams came true, as Joseph said.
Then Pharaoh dreamed some dreams.
'I need some help, some wise man, please,
To tell me what they mean.'

'I met a man,' the cupbearer said,
'When I was locked up tight.
He knew the meaning of my dream.
He got it all just right.'

'Then fetch him!'
PHARAOH told his men.
'Bring him here right now!'
And then, when Joseph came, he said,
'**MY** dream's about ... A COW!'

Joseph dreamed. His brothers SCHEMED.
And when it all was through,
God dreamed Joseph's dream with him.
And Joseph's dream came TRUE.

ANSWERS and FAMINES

Joseph dreamed. His brothers SCHEMED.
And when it all was through,
God dreamed Joseph's dream with him.
And Joseph's dream came TRUE.

'I dreamed that I saw **seven COWS**
Walk out of the Nile.
PLUMP and **black** and beautiful,
They made me want to smile.

'Then seven SKINNY COWS appeared,
Ugly, thin and brown.
They walked up to the healthy cows
And SWALLOWED them all down!

'Then **seven EARS OF GRAIN** appeared,
Rich and good and fat.
But **seven sickly** ears came next
And ATE them, just like that!'

Then Joseph said, 'I understand.
God's made it very plain.
The dreams are one, they are not two.
Their meaning is the same.

BURP!

'The seven cows and ears of grain,
Lovely, PLUMP and **good**,
Are seven years when crops will grow
       And you'll have lots of food.

 'But seven cows and ears of grain,
SICKLY, sad and THIN,
Are seven years of famine with
No harvests to bring in.

'So in those seven fruitful years,
You need to store up wheat.
And when the famine comes, at last,
You'll have enough to eat.

'You need to find some **clever man**
To see this project through.'
Then PHARAOH stared and smiled and said,
'Hey, Joseph, why not you?'

So Joseph went from **prisoner**
To Pharaoh's **right-hand man**,
And started building storehouses
Right across the land.

And in those seven fruitful years,
Joseph stored up wheat.
So when the famine came, the people
Had enough to eat.

But back where Joseph's brothers lived,
The famine also came.
So off to EGYPT they all went
To try and buy some grain.

When Joseph's servants led them in,
He knew just who they were.
But, clueless, every brother bowed
And said, **'Please help us, sir.'**

And that's when Joseph's **dreams came true**,
Of BOWING STARS and GRAIN.
'But have my brothers changed,' he thought.
'Or are they just the same?

'I'll see if they can pass my test,
A test of loyalty.
And if they do, I will reveal
My true identity!'

Joseph dreamed. His brothers SCHEMED.
And when it all was through,
God dreamed Joseph's dream with him.
And Joseph's dream came TRUE.

Famines and Family

Joseph dreamed. His brothers SCHEMED.
And when it all was through,
God dreamed Joseph's dream with him.
And Joseph's dream came **TRUE**.

So Joseph cried, 'You men are **SPIES!**
 Come to search our land,
  And find out all our weaknesses,
  And kill us if you can.'

'**WE'RE NOT!**' they said. 'We're simple men,
With carts to put grain in.
We'll buy some food, then back to Dad
And brother Benjamin.'

'There is another brother, then?'
Joseph asked each one.
'Our Brother Benjamin,' they said.
'And then there's one who's . . . **gone**.'

'Then bring young Benjamin to me.
Bring him here, I say.
And you there,' Joseph added, pointing,
'You will have to stay.'

So Simeon was **bound** and JAILED.
The rest went back to Dad.
The thought of sending Benjamin
Made Jacob very sad.

'I will not lose another son,'
He said, with CRACKING voice.
But when the food ran out again,
He really had no choice.

So off to Egypt they all went,
Benjamin in tow.
They hoped the man would give them grain,
And let their **brother go**.

And that is just what Joseph did.
So Simeon went FREE.
Then Joseph tried just one more time
To test their **loyalty**.

He told his servants, 'Put a cup
In Benjamin's grain sack.
And when they've gone, **arrest them all**,
And force them to come back.'

'YOU THIEVES!' he cried. 'You stole from me,
And someone here must pay.
Whoever has my silver cup
Will stay here as my slave.'

Of course, it was in young Ben's sack.
So Judah bowed his head.
'To lose this boy will kill our dad.
Make me your **slave**, instead.'

And that's the moment Joseph knew
His brothers weren't the same.
They weren't the men who'd torn his coat
    And sold him as a slave.

'IT'S ME!' he cried. 'It's Joseph, see!
  Your brother who was gone.'
The brothers all were terrified,
Remembering what they'd done.

(YOO! HOO! IT'S ME!)

'No need to fear,' he then made clear.
'You meant to **wreck** my dreams.
  But God turned harm, with his strong arm,
To something good, it seems.

'So go to **Canaan**, fetch our dad.
Bring him back with you.
And in this land, we'll trust God's hand
To make our dreams come true.'

Joseph dreamed. His brothers SCHEMED.
And when it all was through,
God dreamed Joseph's dream with him.
And Joseph's dream came **TRUE**.

The BABY in the BASKET

Hush a bye baby in your reed boat,
Down by the bank you **bob** and you **float**.
Sleep and be safe and know, as you do,
Your God and your sister watch over you.

Pharaoh had made God's people his slaves.
Still they grew **STRONG**, and still they grew **BRAVE**.
Fearful they'd rise, rebel and destroy,
He ordered the **death** of each baby boy.

One Hebrew mum came up with a plan
To guard and to save her own little man.
She built him a tiny bulrushes boat,
Caked it in tar, to make the thing float.

Hush a bye baby in your reed boat,
Down by the bank you **bob** and you **float**.
Sleep and be safe and know, as you do,
Your God and your sister watch over you.

Into the boat, her baby boy went.
Following that, his sister was sent
To watch and to care for all of his needs,
Hidden among the Nile river reeds.

Then **Pharaoh's daughter** went for a bath.
Heard something crying, well off the path.
Looked in the river, that's where she spied
The little reed boat with baby inside!

Hush a bye baby in your reed boat,
Down by the bank you **bob** and you **float**.
Sleep and be safe and know, as you do,
Your God and your sister watch over you.

'**Bring him to me,**' she ordered her maid.
Into her arms the baby was laid.
'A Hebrew,' she said, then kindly she smiled.
'I'll raise him as my own dear little child.'

'A nursemaid', she said, 'is what this child needs.'
And that's when his sister *rose from the reeds*.
'I know a woman,' the girl volunteered.
'She'll do a great job. She's living near here.'

The mother was paid to feed her own son,
Then gave him right back when nursing was done.
'His name will be **MOSES**,' announced Pharaoh's daughter.
'The baby I pulled up out of the water!'

Hush a bye baby in your reed boat,
Down by the bank you **bob** and you **float**.
Sleep and be safe and know, as you do,
Your God and your sister watch over **YOU**.

PHARAOH just says 'NO'

Moses said to Pharaoh, 'Let my people go.'
But Pharaoh said to Moses, 'NO! NO! NO!'

So God turned water into **blood**
That filled the River Nile.
The fish all died. The awful smell
Was horrid, sick and **vile**.

Moses said to Pharaoh, 'Let my people go.'
But Pharaoh said to Moses, 'NO! NO! NO!'

So God sent **frogs** upon the land,
Jumping here and there.
They **hopped** in beds and **plopped** in bowls.
The frogs were everywhere!

Moses said to Pharaoh, 'Let my people go.'
But Pharaoh said to Moses, 'NO! NO! NO!'

So God sent **gnats** upon the land.
The people tried to swat 'em.
The insects kept on biting, though,
From head to toe to bottom.

Moses said to Pharaoh, 'Let my people go.'
But Pharaoh said to Moses, 'NO! NO! NO!'

So God sent **flies** to follow gnats,
More itching, biting, swarming.
The scratching just went on and on,
From night-time until morning.

Moses said to Pharaoh, **'Let my people go.'**
But Pharaoh said to Moses, 'NO! NO! NO!"

So God killed every animal
In stable, barn and shed.
The camels and the cows all died,
The donkeys dropped down **dead**.

Moses said to Pharaoh, **'Let my people go.'**
But Pharaoh said to Moses, 'NO! NO! NO!'

So God sent **sores** upon the land.
Boils, raw and red.
It hurt to stand. It hurt to sit.
It hurt to lie in bed.

Moses said to Pharaoh, **'Let my people go.'**
But Pharaoh said to Moses, 'NO! NO! NO!'

So God sent **hailstorms** crashing down
To crush the crops of corn.
And every stalk and every leaf
Was broken, ripped and torn.

Moses said to Pharaoh, 'Let my people go.'
But Pharaoh said to Moses, 'NO! NO! NO!'

So God sent **locusts** on the land
To eat what fruit was there.
They munched and crunched on all the trees
Till every branch was bare.

Moses said to Pharaoh, 'Let my people go.'
But Pharaoh said to Moses, 'NO! NO! NO!'

Then God sent **darkness** like a cloak
To cover the whole place.
They *tripped* and fell.
　　　　　No one could see
Their hand before their face.

Moses said to Pharaoh, 'Let my people go.'
But Pharaoh said to Moses, 'NO! NO! NO!'

So God killed **every firstborn child**
Of Egypt in the night.
But every child of Israel
Lived to see daylight.

Then Moses said to Pharaoh, 'Let my people go.'
And Pharaoh said, 'My son is dead. This is the hardest blow.
So take your people and their things, and go away. Please GO!'

FREE at last

When **PHARAOH** lost his firstborn son,
He said to Moses, 'Leave, please **LEAVE**.
Take your people, every one.
And let us mourn and let us grieve.'

So Moses led his people out.
Free at last, they went their way,
Free to **SING** and free to **SHOUT**,
Free to live free every day.

Then Pharaoh had a change of heart.
'I will **not** let my slaves go **FREE**!'
He climbed into his chariot,
And led his army to the sea.

Six hundred chariots he led.
And countless soldiers followed, too.
The Hebrew people cried and said,
'**MOSES**, now what will you do?'

So God told Moses, 'Trust me, please.
Have no fear, just raise your staff.
I'll part the waters of the sea,
And you will have a clear, safe path.'

So Moses raised his staff up HIGH,
And watched the Red Sea split in TWO.
A wall of water on each side,
Amazed, he led his people through.

But Pharaoh's army still pursued.
He drove his chariots down that path.
Their wheels STUCK in the mud like GLUE.
And that's when Moses dropped his staff.

The sea returned, a mighty rush,
Walls of water CRASHING DOWN.
Then every chariot was Crushed.
And Pharaoh's soldiers all were drowned.

The people cheered, their voices raised.
Cheered, for they, at last, were FREE.
And Moses sang a song of praise
To celebrate the victory.

'Sing to God, to God on high,
For he has won the victory.
See where Pharaoh's chariots lie,
Buried deep beneath the sea.'

Make the WALL small

A **TALL** wall, a **THICK** wall,
A never-fall-at-all wall.
But follow God's call,
And you'll make the wall **SMALL**.

Jericho city was surrounded by a wall
Built big and strong so it would never fall.
But God told Joshua to go inside.
Then he gave him a plan that was quite a surprise.

A **TALL** wall, a **THICK** wall,
A never-fall-at-all wall.
But follow God's call,
And you'll make the wall **SMALL**.

'March once round the city, six days in a row,
The priests in front, and the army in tow,
The ark of the covenant leading the way,
And ram-horn trumpets ready to play.'

A **TALL** wall, a **THICK** wall,
A never-fall-at-all wall.
But follow God's call,
And you'll make the wall **SMALL**.

'On the **seventh day**, march round **seven times**.
Blow **seven trumpets**, LOUD and high.
Then lift your voices, let your shouts ring round,
And Jericho's walls will come tumbling down.'

A TALL wall, a THICK wall,
A never-fall-at-all wall.
But follow God's call,
And you'll make the wall SMALL.

So the people of God did what he asked,
Followed his instructions, completed the task.
And much to their surprise, crazy as it sounds,
Jericho's walls came tumbling down!
Yes, Jericho's walls came tumbling down!

A TALL wall, a THICK wall,
A never-fall-at-all wall.
But follow God's call,
And you'll make the wall SMALL.

TRUMPETS and JARS and TORCHES

Gideon hid in a winepress, **trembling**,
Beating out flour from wheat.
Midian soldiers had conquered his land
And left him with little to eat.

'**Greetings, BRAVE man!**' an angel said.
  Calling into the press,
  'Are you talking to me?' frightened Gideon asked.
    'I think you've confused the address.'

    'You are **chosen by God**,' the angel replied,
'To drive out the Midianites.
So God will be with you each step of the way,
And help you to win this fight.'

'Show me a sign,' **trembling** Gideon begged him.
'I'll put out a sheepskin tonight.
Wet it and soak it, all covered with dew
But leave the ground, round it, dry.'

So God SOAKED the fleece like Gideon said,
Left it sitting upon dry ground.
But unconvinced, Gideon cheekily asked,
'Could you do it the other way round?'

So God wet the ground and left the fleece dry.
And that did the trick for Gideon.
And that's when he went to gather an army,
And lead them in war against Midian.

'I'm sorry,' God said. 'Your army's too BIG.
I want you to trust in me.
So let it be known that **if anyone's scared**,
He can go home as quick as can be.'

Twenty-two thousand soldiers went home.
Gideon wanted to cry.
'I know you won't like this,' God announced,
'But your numbers are **still far too** HIGH.

'Lead all of your soldiers down to the river.
Watch how they take a drink.
Keep only the men who scoop up the water.
Your numbers will certainly SHRINK.'

Just **three hundred men** were all that remained.
Gideon shook his head.
He picked up his sword. **'I'm sorry,'** said God.
'I've got better weapons, instead.

'Give all of your men a TRUMPET, and hide
A TORCH in a big clay jar.
Then go to the enemy camp, late at night,
And that's where we'll win this war.'

So Gideon went to the Midian camp,
And every man broke his JAR.
And torches shone bright and trumpets BLEW LOUD,
Frightening and bizarre.

The Midianites were surprised and bewildered,
And swinging their SWORDS about
Finished up fighting, confused, with each other,
Taking their own men out!

So Gideon ended up winning that night,
An unlikely battle star,
With three hundred men and one great big God,
And trumpets and torches and jars.

Trumpets and jars and torches.
Trumpets and torches and jars.
Those are the weapons that God gave Gideon,
TRUMPETS and TORCHES and JARS.

HAIR, HAIR, EVERYWHERE!

HAIR, HAIR, EVERYWHERE.
Samson had a lot of hair.
Dark and **twirly**, **long** and **curly**,
Samson loved his hair.

Samson was a Nazirite,
Which means he made a vow
To never let a RAZOR CUT
The hair from off his brow,

Or let a drop of alcohol
Trickle down his throat,
Or snack on unclean animals,
Like camel, pig or stoat.

So God made him a promise,
'I'll make you BIG and STRONG,
Assuming that you keep your vow,
And let your hair grow long.'

HAIR, HAIR, EVERYWHERE.
Samson had a lot of hair.
Tangled truly, quite **unruly**,
Samson loved his hair.

Everyone in Israel
Feared the Philistines,
So Samson used his MIGHTY STRENGTH
To keep them all in line.

He caught three hundred foxes,
Tied torches 'tween their tails
Then sent them running through the fields
To burn up their hay bales.

The Philistines came back at him
With knives and spears and STONES.
Samson killed a thousand of them
With a donkey bone!

HAIR, HAIR, EVERYWHERE.
Samson had a lot of hair.
Soft and fluffy, rather scruffy,
Samson loved his hair.

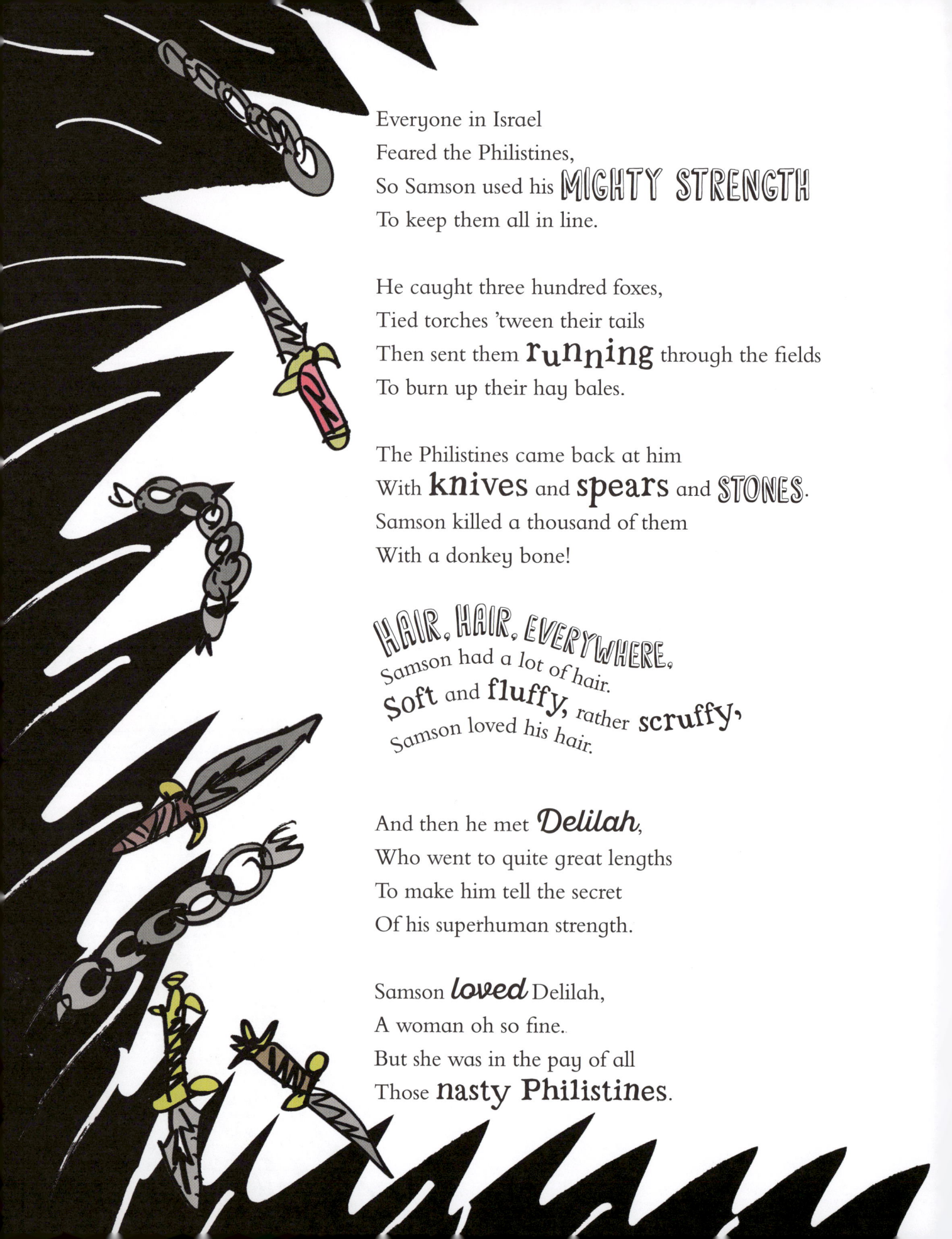

And then he met Delilah,
Who went to quite great lengths
To make him tell the secret
Of his superhuman strength.

Samson loved Delilah,
A woman oh so fine.
But she was in the pay of all
Those nasty Philistines.

He told Delilah lots of **lies**
To lead them all astray,
Until she begged and pleaded,
One last fateful day.

HAIR, HAIR, EVERYWHERE.
Samson had a lot of hair.
Thick and **black,** on arms and back,
Samson loved his hair.

'Just cut my hair,' he told her.
'And then you'll understand.
I'll lose my strength and soon become
As WEAK as any man.'

When Samson fell asleep, that night
Delilah cut his **locks**.
The Philistines BURST in the room,
And Samson was quite shocked.

They tied him up with heavy chains.
They put his eyes out too.
But Samson could do nothing,
Without his long hairdo.

HAIR, HAIR, NOT ANYWHERE.
Samson lost his head of hair.
Shaven now, a broken vow,
Samson had no hair.

They made him push a millstone
To grind grain into flour,
But slowly Samson's hair grew back,
Hour after hour.

They **dragged** him to their temple
To mock him and make fun.
They stood him between pillars.
Chained up, he couldn't run.

But with his hair, his strength returned.
So Samson pushed and cried.
The pillars cracked, the place collapsed,
And everybody died.

HAIR, HAIR, EVERYWHERE.
Samson once again had hair.
Rinse, repeat, bad guys **defeat!**
Samson **LOVED** his hair.

SOMEBODY'S calling MY NAME

'Old Eli, did you CALL me?
Loud and clear and plain?
Oh, Eli, I just heard a voice
Shouting out my NAME!'

Blind Eli was a priest.
And Samuel was a lad,
Who helped the priest each day
With every job he had.
Together they served God,
Inside the holy tent.
When Samuel's bedtime came,
That's also where he went.

And then, one night, the boy
Heard someone call his name.
It **frightened** him, it did!
He got up, just the same.
He went to Eli, quick,
And whispered in his ear,
As clearly as he could,
So old Eli could hear:

'Old Eli, did you CALL me?
Loud and clear and plain?
Oh, Eli, I just heard a voice
Shouting out my NAME!'

Old Eli rubbed his eyes.
Old Eli shook his head.
'It wasn't me, my boy.
Now hurry off to bed.'
So Samuel **scurried** back,
Cold shivers down his spine,
Pulled the covers over
And hoped that he'd be fine.

But as he nodded off,
The voice called out once more.
He FELL right out of bed,
And landed on the floor.
He ran right back to Eli,
And shouted in his ear,
As plainly as he could,
So old Eli could hear.

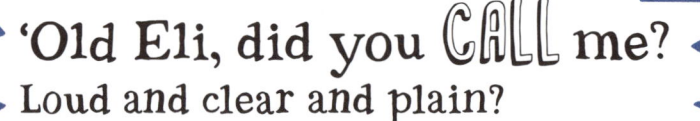

'Old Eli, did you CALL me?
Loud and clear and plain?
Oh, Eli, I just heard a voice
Shouting out my NAME!'

Eli was not happy.
Old Eli was annoyed.
'It wasn't me, I told you!
GO BACK TO BED, MY BOY!'
So Samuel slipped away.
On tippy-toes he went,
Watching every shadow
That danced around the tent.

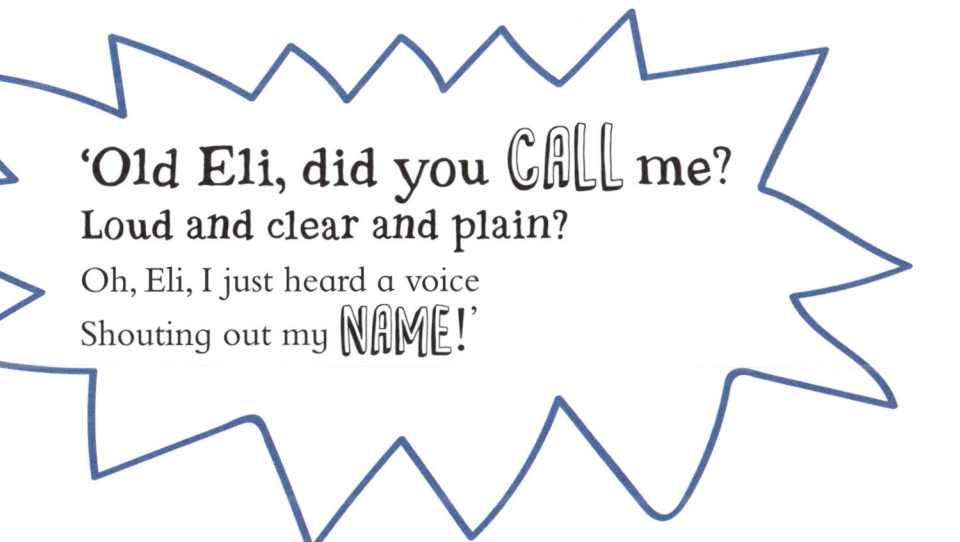

But when he hit the bed
Again he heard that voice.
Back he flew to Eli.
'I really had no choice.
Please don't say you're angry,'
He shouted through his tears.
'It's calling me again.
I heard it loud and clear!'

'Old Eli, did you CALL me?
Loud and clear and plain?
Oh, Eli, I just heard a voice
Shouting out my NAME!'

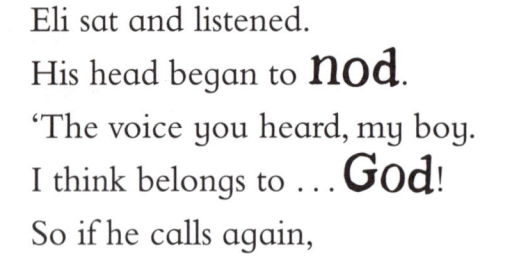

Eli sat and listened.
His head began to **nod**.
'The voice you heard, my boy.
I think belongs to . . . **God**!
So if he calls again,
Don't worry and don't fear.
Just answer him and say,

"Speak, Lord, your servant hears."'

So that's what Samuel did,
When next he heard his name.
God gave the boy a message.
And PROPHECIES just came
To Samuel all his life,
As boy grew into man.
He heard the things God said,
And spread them through the land.

'Old Eli, did you CALL me?
Loud and clear and plain?
Oh, Eli, I just heard a voice
Shouting out my NAME!'

When my FEARS are GIANT-SIZED

David took his brothers
A lunch of cheese and bread.
Soldiers on a battlefield,
They needed to be fed.
That's when he spied a GIANT foot
And leg and arm and head
And heard the giant's challenge
And bravely stood and said:

'God helped me **beat a LION**.
God helped me **beat a BEAR**.
So when my fears are GIANT-SIZED,
I trust that God is there.'

'You cannot fight that GIANT!'
His frightened brothers cried.
'He'll **squash** you like an insect.
He's more than twice your size.
You're just a little shepherd boy.
You should be terrified!'
But David knew that God would help
And that's why he replied:

'God helped me **beat** a LION.
God helped me **beat** a BEAR.
So when my fears are GIANT-SIZED,
I trust that God is there.'

So David went and told the king,
'I'll take that giant's dare.'
'Then have my armour,' said the king.
'It's standing over there.'
When David tried it on
He found it much too hard to wear.
'A sling and stones is all I need,'
He said. 'Well, and a prayer!'

'God helped me **beat** a LION.
God helped me **beat** a BEAR.
So when my fears are GIANT-SIZED,
I trust that God is there.'

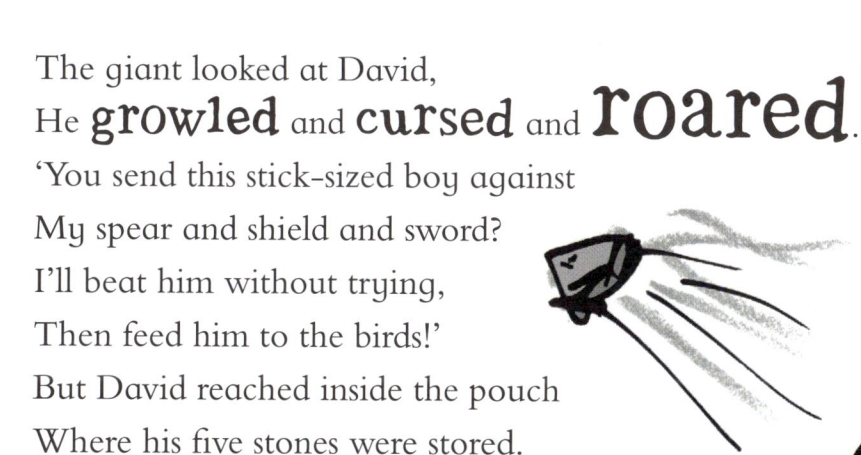

The giant looked at David,
He **growled** and **cursed** and **roared**.
'You send this stick-sized boy against
My spear and shield and sword?
I'll beat him without trying,
Then feed him to the birds!'
But David reached inside the pouch
Where his five stones were stored.

'God helped me **beat a LION**.
God helped me **beat a BEAR**.
So when my fears are **GIANT**-SIZED,
I trust that God is there.'

The giant rushed towards him,
His face an ANGRY RED.
David swung his sling and aimed
Straight for the giant's head.
That small stone struck its target.
The giant fell down dead.
And as his brothers clapped and cheered,
David simply said:

'God helped me **beat a LION**.
God helped me **beat a BEAR**.
So when my fears are **GIANT**-SIZED,
I trust that God is there.'

SWALLOWED

The Ninevites were **nasty**. They were **CRUEL** and no good.
God sent his prophet, Jonah, to tell them where they stood.
'Change your evil ways, and turn your lives around.
I'll give you fifty days, then I'll knock your city down.'

But Jonah wasn't happy when God gave him this news.
He feared the men of Nineveh. He hated them, too.
He decided not to tell them about God's gracious plan.
And hoped God would destroy them, every woman and man.

JONAH learned the **HARD WAY**
That God is in control,
That hating is not great,
And it will **SWALLOW** you whole!

So off he went to Tarshish, on board a foreign ship,
As far away from Nineveh as he could sneak and slip.
But God was watching anyway, and sent a **mighty GALE**.
And Jonah was thrown overboard and swallowed by a whale.

He waited there for three long days, and that is when he knew
That God gave him a second chance to do what he should do.
So Jonah prayed a 'sorry' prayer, admitted God was right,
And when the whale had spat him out, went to the Ninevites.

JONAH learned the HARD WAY
That God is in control,
That hating is not great,
And it will SWALLOW you whole!

So Jonah told the Ninevites the thing that God had planned.
The Ninevites said 'sorry', every woman and man.
But Jonah was not happy, his heart still filled with hate.
He muttered and he moaned, for he knew God's love was great.

'I knew that you would save them,' Jonah grumbled to God.
And God replied, 'But Jonah tell me why you think that's odd.
I offer my forgiveness, for that is my delight,
Even to a people that does not know wrong from right.'

JONAH learned the HARD WAY
That God is in control,
That hating is not great,
And it will SWALLOW you whole!

DARK and DAMP and DEEP

Daniel helped the mighty King
With any problem he might bring.
He gave advice on everything
The King would set before him.

But Daniel had some enemies,
Overwhelmed with jealousy,
Who made an evil plan to see
If they could trap and kill him.

The den was DARK and DAMP and DEEP.
The lions growled and roared and leaped.
But Daniel got a good night's sleep,
For God was in there with him.

'Let's make a law to plainly say
That to the King we all must pray.
And then, when Daniel disobeys,
Our chance will come to catch him.

'For anyone who breaks the law
Will end up in the lions' paws,
Crushed between the lions' jaws.
And that will surely end him.'

The den was DARK and DAMP and DEEP.
The lions **growled** and roared and leaped.
But Daniel got a good night's sleep,
For God was in there with him.

So off they went to see the King.
And he agreed to everything.
It made him proud to think they'd bring
Their sacred prayers before him.

But then when Daniel disobeyed,
And bowed his head to God and prayed,
The King was sad and so dismayed,
For he would have to kill him.

The den was DARK and DAMP and DEEP.
The lions **growled** and roared and leaped.
But Daniel got a good night's sleep,
For God was in there with him.

So, in the den poor Daniel dropped.
The lions roared and licked their chops.
And then quite suddenly they stopped,
As someone came to save him.

It was an angel, bright and white,
Who gave the lions such a fright.
He shut their mouths. He shut them tight,
While Daniel sat and watched him.

The den was DARK and DAMP and DEEP.
The lions **growled** and **roared** and **leaped**.
But Daniel got a good night's sleep,
For God was in there with him.

And when the king called down next day,
Daniel answered back to say
That God had answered when he prayed,
And found a way to save him.

The king was thrilled and so he said
'Bring Daniel up. He is not dead.
Drop down his enemies, instead,
And let the lions eat them!'

The den was DARK and DAMP and DEEP.
The lions **growled** and **roared** and **leaped**.
But Daniel got a good night's sleep,
For God was in there with him.

If I DIE, I DIE

Esther was a lovely woman, **beautiful** in fact.
A star addition to the King's ha-reem.
So when the king went looking for a new, replacement wife,
He settled on young Esther as his queen.

Esther was an orphan, so her uncle Mordecai
Had raised her like a daughter, **brave** and *true*.
'Our people have been captives here,' he told her, 'so beware.
Don't let the King know that you are a Jew.'

A-HAS-U-E-RUS was the King of Persians and of Medes,
His name a mouthful, even in that land.
He had no clue his wife was Jewish, so things got quite strange
When Haman came to see him, with a plan.

HAMAN was his right-hand man, vengeful, cruel and proud,
Who thought he had been snubbed by Mordecai.
'These Jews are trouble, Majesty,' is what he told the King.
'I think it's time that all of them should die.'

The King agreed, not knowing that poor Esther would die, too.
So happy Haman made his way back home,
And built a **gallows** in his garden, just for Mordecai,
Between the **water feature** and the **GNOMES**.

When Mordecai found out, he hurried straight to Esther's house.
'**HAMAN PLANS TO WIPE OUT OUR WHOLE RACE!**
You and you alone can stop this awful crime my dear.
Go and tell the King and plead our case.'

'But, Uncle, I can't see the King unless he asks me in,'
Esther **trembled** back her sad reply.
'If I go uninvited, then the King can have me **KILLED**.
The chance is very high that I could die!'

'Do you believe that you will live if Haman has his way?
You'll disappear like us without a trace.
You're in the palace for a reason,' argued Mordecai.
'To be God's hero in this time and place.'

'I'll do it, then,' said Esther, **'and if I die, I DIE.'**

So in she went, an uninvited guest.
Ahasuerus took his time, and when he finally spoke,
Esther's heart was **THUMPING** in her chest.

'Come in, my dear,' he said, at last. 'What can I do for you?'
'Let's host a banquet,' Esther said, relieved.
'And let's ask Haman. He would make a lovely dinner guest.
We'll honour him with all he should receive.'

Haman was delighted to have dinner with the *Queen*,
But Esther's words soon filled him with dismay.
'Someone wants to kill me, dear,' she notified the King.
'And all my fellow Jews, I'm sad to say.'

Ahasuerus shouted, **'TELL ME NOW, WHO IS THIS MAN?'**
And Haman tried to sink into his seat.
'It's him,' said Esther, finger pointed right at Haman's face.
'The man we have invited, here, to eat.'

'GUARDS!' Ahasuerus ordered. 'Take that man away!
And let the Jews live happy in their homes.'
So only Haman died that day, hanged on his *gallows* high,
Between the *water feature* and the **GNOMES**.

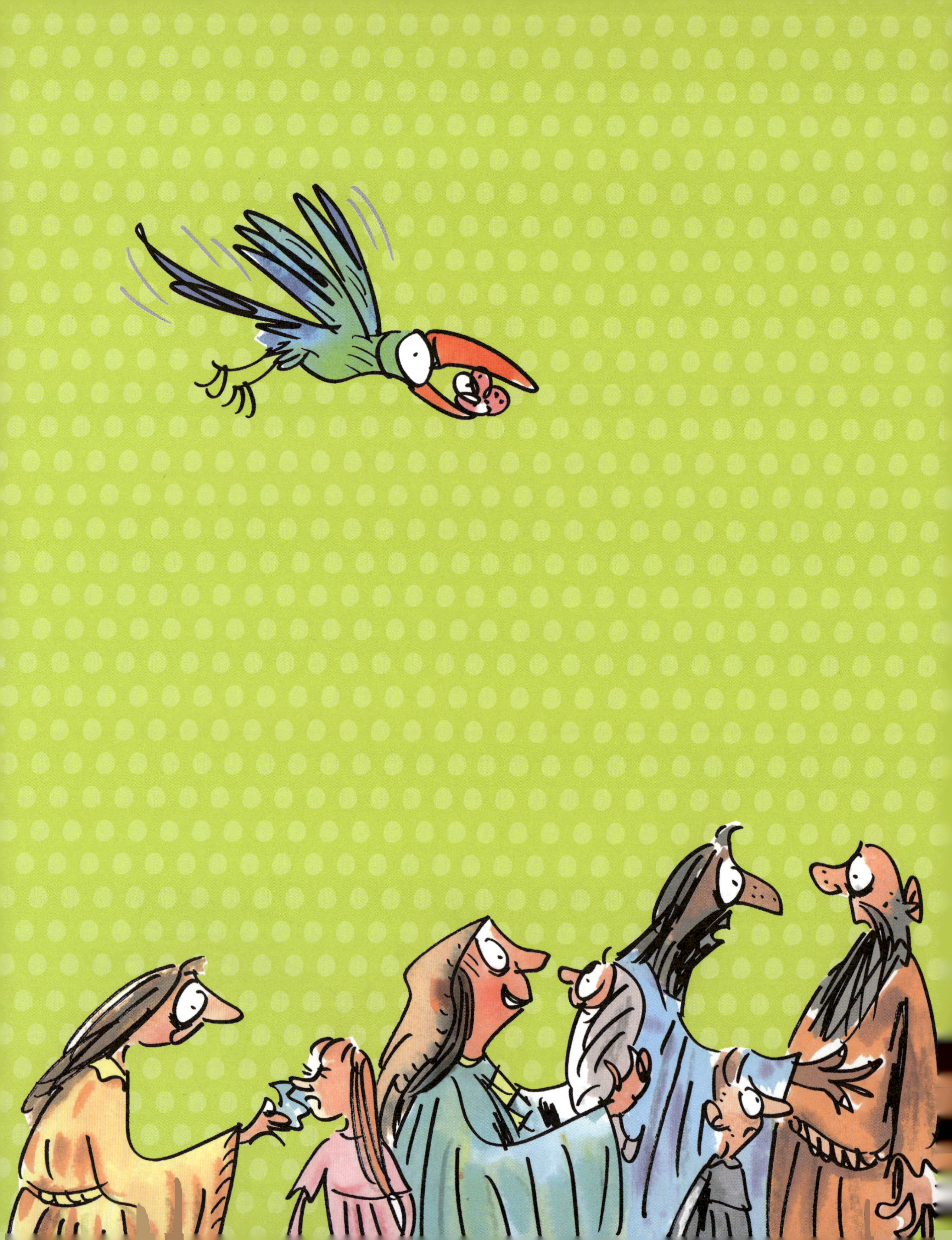

NEW TESTAMENT STORIES

A WOMAN called MARY

A woman called Mary
Was doing her chores,
When an angel arrived,
But not through the doors.
He simply appeared
And she dropped to the floor.
'Hello, Mary,' he said.
'GOD IS WITH YOU.'

'God is with me?' She wondered.
'But what does that mean?
What's this all about?
Is it some kind of dream?'
The angel just smiled.
'Don't be scared. Please don't scream.
God is happy with you
AND WILL BLESS YOU!'

God **knocks** down the proud,
And **lifts** up the meek,
And does mighty things
For those who are weak.
And blesses the ones
Whose service he seeks.
So sing out his praise,
HE'S AMAZING!

'You'll soon have a baby,'
The angel went on.
'A quite special baby
Called *Jesus*, God's Son.
The heir of King David,
He'll sit on his throne.
And his kingdom
WILL LAST FOR EVER.'

'But how?' Mary asked.
'I don't understand.
I'm engaged to be wed
But he's not yet my man.'
'Trust God,' said the angel.
'He's got it all planned.
His *Spirit* will
COME UPON YOU.'

God **knocks** down the proud,
And *lifts* up the meek,
And does mighty things
For those who are weak.
And blesses the ones
Whose service he seeks.
So sing out his praise,
HE'S AMAZING!

'GOD'S OWN HOLY SON
Is the child you will bear.

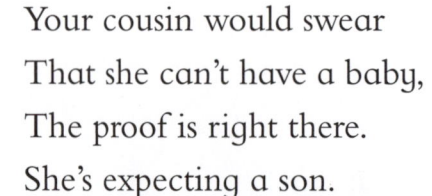

Impossible? NO!

Your cousin would swear
That she can't have a baby,
The proof is right there.
She's expecting a son.
GO AND SEE HER.

'THERE'S NOTHING THAT GOD

Cannot do, don't you see?'
'Well, then,' Mary nodded,
'Please do that for me,
This impossible thing.
His servant I'll be.'
Then the angel waved 'BYE'.
And he left her.

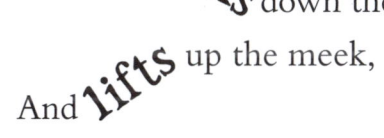

God **knocks** down the proud,
And **lifts** up the meek,
And does mighty things
For those who are weak.
And blesses the ones
Whose service he seeks.
So sing out his praise,

HE'S AMAZING!

JOSEPH, don't worry

JOSEPH don't worry, JOSEPH don't weep.
Lay down your head, and go back to sleep.
Mary's been faithful. Her love's strong and deep,
And her baby is *God's own son*.

All night, Joseph **tossed**. All night, Joseph **turned**.
He just couldn't sleep. He'd only just learned
That Mary was pregnant. What's more, she'd confirmed
That the baby she bore was not his.

She'd told him this tale: an angelic visit,
A son to be born by God's Holy Spirit.
The more she went on, the less he believed it.
He wanted to break their engagement.

JOSEPH don't worry, JOSEPH don't weep.
Lay down your head, and go back to sleep.
Mary's been faithful. Her love's strong and deep,
And her baby is *God's own son*.

But just as sleep came, that **angel** appeared.
'Don't worry,' he said, 'there's nothing to fear.
I know that you're troubled, so you need to hear
That Mary is telling the truth.

'The baby she bears is God's holy son.
Call his name **JESUS**, for he is the one
God promised to send to save everyone.
Immanuel. God is with us!'

JOSEPH don't worry, **JOSEPH** don't weep.
Lay down your head, and go back to sleep.
Mary's been faithful. Her love's strong and deep,
And her baby is *God's own son*.

'He's the answer to all that the prophets have said.
So keep your engagement. Be glad and be wed.'
And when Joseph woke up, that's just what he did.
He took Mary to be his wife.

JOSEPH don't worry, **JOSEPH** don't weep.
Lay down your head, and go back to sleep.
Mary's been faithful. Her love's strong and deep,
And her baby is *God's own son*.

It begins in BETHLEHEM

Shepherds lying on a hill.
The night was silent, all was still.
They watched their flock of grazing sheep,
And tried hard not to fall asleep,

When, **BRIGHT** and white, an angel came
To light the night, a *fiery flame*.
The shepherds trembled where they lay.
The angel said, 'Don't be afraid.'

Sing praise to God and give him glory.
Celebrate his wondrous story
Of love and joy and peace to men,
For it begins in BETHLEHEM.

'The news is good, the news I bring.
Good news to make you leap and *sing*.
Good news for people everywhere.
Good news of joy for all to share.

'Good news, for God has kept his word,
And sent his saviour, Christ the Lord.
The one he promised he would send
Is born this day in BETHLEHEM.'

Sing praise to God and give him glory.
Celebrate his wondrous story
Of love and joy and peace to men,
For it begins in BETHLEHEM.

'And this will be a sign for you.
This is how you'll know it's true.
You'll find a baby wrapped in cloth,
Sleeping in a cattle trough.'

The angel, then, was joined by more,
Six and twelve and twenty-four,
And then too many more to number,
A heaven-choir, LOUD AS THUNDER.

Sing praise to God and give him glory.
Celebrate his wondrous story
Of love and joy and peace to men,
For it begins in BETHLEHEM.

And so the angels left that place,
Just like they'd come, without a trace,
Except for all they sang and said,
Which echoed in the shepherds' heads.

'Let's go to Bethlehem and see,'
The shepherds all, as one, agreed.
They found the baby where he lay,
Asleep upon a bed of hay.

Sing praise to God and give him glory.
Celebrate his wondrous story
Of love and joy and peace to men,
For it begins in BETHLEHEM.

They told them what the angels said.
Then Mary smiled and raised her head.
A secret hid there, in her eyes,
For she was not one bit surprised.

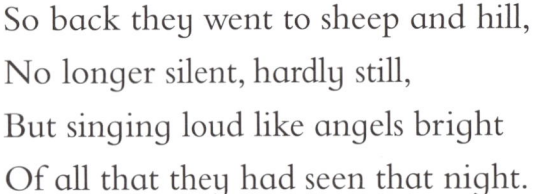

So back they went to sheep and hill,
No longer silent, hardly still,
But singing loud like angels bright
Of all that they had seen that night.

Sing praise to God and give him glory.
Celebrate his wondrous story
Of love and joy and peace to men,
For it begins in BETHLEHEM.

One HUMP, two HUMPS

The star-watchers watched the stars go by,
Looking for secrets in the sky.
And then they saw a special star,
Away in the west. Away off far.

'A king's been born! That's what it means.
Judea way, or so it seems.'
They climbed aboard their camel-y beasts
And set off west from their homes back east.

One HUMP, two HUMPS, lumpety-lump,
The star-watchers went with a BUMP and a THUMP.
One HUMP, two HUMPS, lumpety-lump,
The star-watchers followed the star.

At last their journey came to an end.
They parked their camels in Jerusalem.
Then they went to Herod, king of the nation,
To ask him for some information.

'Oh king,' they asked. They were quite polite.
'Somewhere, round here, on this starry night,
A brand new baby king abides.
Can you tell us where this child resides?'

One HUMP, two HUMPS, lumpety-lump,
The star-watchers went with a BUMP and a THUMP.
One HUMP, two HUMPS, lumpety-lump,
The star-watchers followed the star.

A worried look crossed Herod's face.
He had no plans to be replaced.
So he asked his priests if they could tell
Where this brand new baby king might dwell.

The priests all answered straight away.
'BETHLEHEM is what the prophets say.'
Then Herod thought an evil thing.
'I think I need to meet this king.'

One HUMP, two HUMPS, lumpety-lump,
The star-watchers went with a BUMP and a THUMP.
One HUMP, two HUMPS, lumpety-lump,
The star-watchers followed the star.

'Star-watchers, friends,' King Herod smiled.
'In Bethlehem you'll find the child.
Would you tell me where you find him, please?
The exact address would put my mind at ease.'

Herod, of course, told them a lie.
He'd already planned for the child to die.
When he found the boy, that's what he'd do.
So the star-watchers left, without a clue.

One HUMP, two HUMPS, lumpety-lump,
The star-watchers went with a BUMP and a THUMP.
One HUMP, two HUMPS, lumpety-lump,
The star-watchers followed the star.

The **shining star** led them to the place.
A simple house, not some fancy space.
And when they saw the little boy,
They gave him a pile of special 'toys'.

Presents, rather, fit for a king.
A bunch of shiny golden things.
A spice called myrrh, a sort of perfume.
While smelly frankincense filled the room.

Then, in the night, they had a dream
That showed them Herod's evil scheme.
So they never said where the boy's house lay
But went straight home by another way.

One HUMP, two HUMPS, lumpety-lump,
The star-watchers went with a BUMP and a THUMP.
One HUMP, two HUMPS, lumpety-lump,
The star-watchers followed the star.

Fill in all the Valleys

John lived in the **wilderness**.
He was a sight to see.
He dressed himself in camel skins,
Ate locusts for his tea.

'GET READY!' was his message.
'Change your wicked ways.
For God is sending someone
Who will leave you all amazed.'

'Fill in all the valleys.
KNOCK the mountains **down**.
Straighten out the highways,
God is coming to town.'

And then he told the people
Exactly what to do:
'Soldiers, don't be greedy
And tax collectors, too.'

'And all of you must help the poor,
Must give, and play your part,
Be baptized in the river,
As a sign of your new start.'

'Fill in all the valleys.
KNOCK the mountains **down**.
Straighten out the highways,
God is coming to town.'

Then Jesus, just as promised,
Walked right through the crowd.
'This is him – the **Lamb of God!**'
John called out, clear and loud.

Then Jesus asked to be baptized
But John did not agree.
'If anyone should baptize, here,
Then you should baptize me!'

'Fill in all the valleys.
KNOCK the mountains down.
Straighten out the highways,
God is coming to town.'

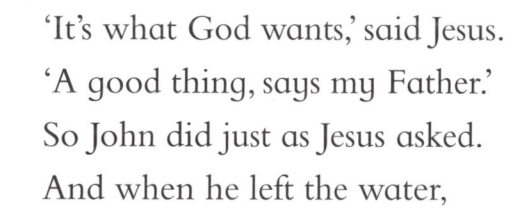

'It's what God wants,' said Jesus.
'A good thing, says my Father.'
So John did just as Jesus asked.
And when he left the water,

The Holy Spirit like a dove
Appeared on Jesus' head.
'Here is my beloved son,'
God's voice, from heaven, said.

'Fill in all the valleys.
KNOCK the mountains down.
Straighten out the highways,
God is coming to town.'

Come and follow ME

Brother ONE, brother TWO,
Fishing in the sea.
Brother THREE, brother FOUR,
Come and follow me.

Jesus walked along the shore,
The shore of *Galilee*,
And there he saw two brothers,
Fishing in the sea.

'Leave your nets,' said Jesus.
'Leave them, let them be.
Come and fish for people.
Come and follow me.'

Brother ONE, brother TWO,
Fishing in the sea.
Brother THREE, brother FOUR,
Come and follow me.

So Simon left his nets behind,
Left them by the sea.
Andrew did the same and shouted,
'Hang on, wait for me!'

Then off they went with Jesus,
On the shores of Galilee.
And there they met some other brothers,
Fishing in the sea.

Brother ONE, brother TWO,
Fishing in the sea.
Brother THREE, brother FOUR,
Come and follow me.

Those brothers were called James and John,
The sons of Zebedee.
And Jesus said to them, as well,
'Come and follow me.'

Like that, they left their father,
Surprised as he could be,
And left their nets behind, as well,
Sitting by the sea.

Brother ONE, brother TWO,
Fishing in the sea.
Brother THREE, brother FOUR,
Come and follow me.

ONE friend, TWO friends, THREE friends, FOUR

ONE friend, TWO friends, THREE friends, FOUR
Climbed on a roof and there they tore
A hole as big as a man and more
To lower their fifth friend on the floor.

Jesus was teaching in that place.
The house was full, there was **no space**.
And you should have seen the owner's face,
When his roof disappeared, without a trace.

The four men then apologized,
'Our friend can't move, he's paralysed.
But we think that if Jesus tries,
He can make our friend arise.'

'**Your sins are forgiven!**' Jesus said,
As he looked at the man on his dropdown bed.
But all four friends just scratched their heads.
They thought he'd fix his legs, instead.

The priests were ANGRY, bothered and HOT.
'God alone forgives,' they thought.
'And this man Jesus? God he's not.'
Then Jesus put them on the spot.

'Forgiving sins? That's hard to see.
To prove that God has given me
Such power and authority,
I'll set this poor man's body free.

'Rise and walk,' he told the man.
'Then pick your bed up with your hand.'
And just like that, the man could stand,
And WALK and RUN and JUMP and LAND!

The four friends broke out in a cheer.
One shed a happy little tear.
The crowd praised God and called out clear,
'We've never seen anything like that here!'

ONE friend, TWO friends, THREE friends, FOUR,
Climbed on a roof and there they tore
A hole as big as a man and more
To lower their fifth friend on the floor.

Rumbling Tummies

Jesus was teaching, way up on a hill,
When everyone started **grumbling**.
'The town's far away!
We've been here all day!
And everyone's TUMMY is **rumbling**.
Everyone's TUMMY is **rumbling**.'

'Find them something to eat,' he said to his friends.
'But where?' they all answered, **mumbling**.
'It will take lots of cash,
Yes, quite a big stash,
To stop all these TUMMIES **rumbling**,
To stop all these TUMMIES **rumbling**.'

'A boy here,' said Andrew, 'gave me his lunch.'
And passed it to Jesus, **fumbling**.
Jesus just said,
'Two fish and some bread?
It's enough to stop TUMMIES **rumbling**.
Enough to stop TUMMIES **rumbling**.'

Jesus thanked God, then tore up the cod,
And the bread, too, the whole lot crumbling.
'Sit folk on the ground,
Then pass it around,
And we'll stop all these TUMMIES rumbling.
We'll stop all these TUMMIES rumbling.'

So they carried that food all around the hill,
Rushing and running and stumbling.
From one little lunch,
Jesus fed the whole bunch,
Till nobody's TUMMY was rumbling.
Nobody's TUMMY was rumbling.

There were leftovers, too. Twelve baskets in all,
Stacked so high that they nearly went tumbling.
FIVE THOUSAND, at least
Shared in that feast

With nobody's TUMMY left rumbling.
With nobody's TUMMY left rumbling.

Every last SON

A man had two sons, and he **loved them**,
but one of them went astray.
Took half the man's cash,
And made a **mad dash**
To a country far, far away.

The son went and spent all his money.
He gambled and PARTIED all day.
It didn't take long,
And when it was gone,
His 'friends' all just wandered away.

For **every last SON** *is special*,
No matter how far he roams.
So the father will wait
Just as long as it takes,
Until his lost son comes HOME.

And then when things couldn't look harder,
A famine came on that land.
With nothing to eat,
No shoes on his feet,
The son hoped for some helping hand.

When no one would stoop to assist him,
He found a **disgusting** job,
Feeding the swine.
He wished he could dine
On the grub they sucked into their gobs.

For **every last SON** *is special*,
No matter how far he roams.
So the father will wait
Just as long as it takes,
Until his lost son comes HOME.

And then the son came to his senses.
'Just what am I doing?' he said.
'I'll go to my dad,
Admit I've been bad,
And work as his servant, instead.'

At once, he went back to his father.
And when the old man saw his boy,
He started to **run**
Towards his lost son,
Racing and *jumping* for JOY!

For **every last** SON *is special*,
No matter how far he roams.
So the father will wait
Just as long as it takes,
Until his lost son comes HOME.

And there in the arms of his father,
The son, just as planned, bowed his head.
'I'm not worthy, Dad,
To be called your lad.
Let me work as your servant, instead.'

But the father just smiled and said, 'NONSENSE.'
He called to his servants, 'Come here!
Bring a robe, now!
Go kill a FAT COW.
My lost son has just reappeared!'

'NOT FAIR!' said the older son, grumbling.
'But right,' said his patient old dad.
'Your brother was dead,
He's alive now, instead.
It's time for us all to be glad!'

For every last SON is special,
No matter how far he roams.
So the father will wait
Just as long as it takes,
Until his lost son comes HOME.

Sow, sow, sow your Seeds

Sow, sow, sow your Seeds,
Gently on the ground.
Which will GROW, and which will not,
And where will *fruit* be found?

'A farmer went to sow his seeds,'
Said Jesus, one fine day.
'He threw them here, he threw them there,
He threw them every way!

'Now some seeds fell upon the path.
They BOUNCED and ROLLED around.
So birds swooped down, with hungry cries,
And swallowed them all down.'

Sow, sow, sow your Seeds,
Gently on the ground.
Which will GROW, and which will not,
And where will *fruit* be found?

'And some seeds fell among the rocks,
And then began to sprout,
But WITHERED in the shallow soil,
When the sun came out.'

SOW, SOW, SOW your SEEDS,
Gently on the ground.
Which will GROW, and which will not,
And where will fruit be found?

'And some seeds fell among the weeds.
They grew there, side by side,
Until the SHARP thorns strangled them,
And every seedling died.'

SOW, SOW, SOW your SEEDS,
Gently on the ground.
Which will GROW, and which will not,
And where will fruit be found?

'But some seeds fell on fertile ground,
And soon began to grow,
And gave good fruit, a hundred times
More than what was sown!'

SOW, SOW, SOW your SEEDS,
Gently on the ground.
Which will **GROW**, and which will not,
And where will *fruit* be found?

Then Jesus' friends all came to him,
Questions in their mouths.
'We're puzzled by your story.
Just what is it about?'

'The seed stands for **God's kingdom**,'
Jesus then explained.
'The ground is like the **human heart**.
No one's quite the same.

'Some hearts are like the **hardened path**.
And when they hear God's news,
They simply do not understand.
They walk away confused.

'And that, my friends, is just the time
The **DEVIL** comes to play.
And much like all those greedy birds,
He steals the truth away.

'Some hearts are like the **rocky** ground.
God's truth takes hold at first.
But **WITHERS** up, when life gets hard
And goes from bad to worse.

'Some hearts are like the **thorny** ground,
Where worries, weed-like grow,
And **choke** out peace and **choke** out joy,
Till all the goodness goes.

'But some are like the fertile ground.
And when God's truth takes root
It grows into a *lovely tree*,
BURSTING rich with fruit!'

SOW, SOW, SOW your SEEDS.
Gently on the ground.
Which will **GROW**, and which will not,
And where will *fruit* be found?

Every last LAMB

A shepherd had a hundred sheep
But one of them wandered away.
Was she lost in a **bog**?
Was she chased by a **dog**?
It's really quite hard to say.

For **every last LAMB** *is special*
And no sheep should be left alone.
So the shepherd will make
Any trip he must take
To bring his lost sheep back HOME.

The shepherd set off in a hurry
And left ninety-nine sheep behind.
He climbed over hills,
Took a couple of SPILLS,
Fell hard on his head and behind.

For **every last LAMB** *is special*
And no sheep should be left alone.
So the shepherd will make
Any trip he must take
To bring his lost sheep back HOME.

As night turned to day, he found her.
His sheep was so sad and forlorn.
No sign of a **bog**,
No mad, BARKING **dog**.
She was trapped in a bush full of **THORNS**.

For **every last** LAMB *is special*
And no sheep should be left alone.
So the shepherd will make
Any trip he must take
To bring his lost sheep back HOME.

He carried her to the sheepfold
And, gently, he set her down.
Then he called to his mates,
'Let's all CELEBRATE,
My sheep that was lost is now found!'

For **every last** LAMB *is special*
And no sheep should be left alone.
So the shepherd will make
Any trip he must take
To bring his lost sheep back HOME.

Waiting in LINE

The children were **running** and JUMPING and giggling.
The children were skipping and PLAYING and wiggling.
The children were hopping and SQUIRMING and wriggling,
Waiting in line to see Jesus.

The mothers were wiping their kids' runny noses.
The mothers were stood in a bunch of bored poses.
The mothers, impatiently tapping their toes-es,
Waiting in line to see Jesus.

The fathers were **mumbling** and **moaning** and **SQUAWKING**.
The fathers were **scheming** and **planning** and **TALKING**.
The fathers all **grumbled** about the queue **STOPPING**,
Waiting in line to see Jesus.

Then Jesus' disciples arrived, and explaining,
Said, 'Jesus can't see you. There's no use complaining.
He's healing the sick – there's so many remaining,
Waiting in line to see Jesus.'

'Now stop that,' said Jesus, 'I want the kids near me.
You all should be like them, with no need to fear me.
No waiting,' he said, and he said it quite clearly.
Waiting in line to see Jesus.

So the children **JUMPED** up on his lap and he blessed them.
The mothers all **clapped**, for his words had impressed them.
The fathers clapped too, for the whole thing had stressed them,
Waiting in line to see Jesus.
Waiting in line to see Jesus.

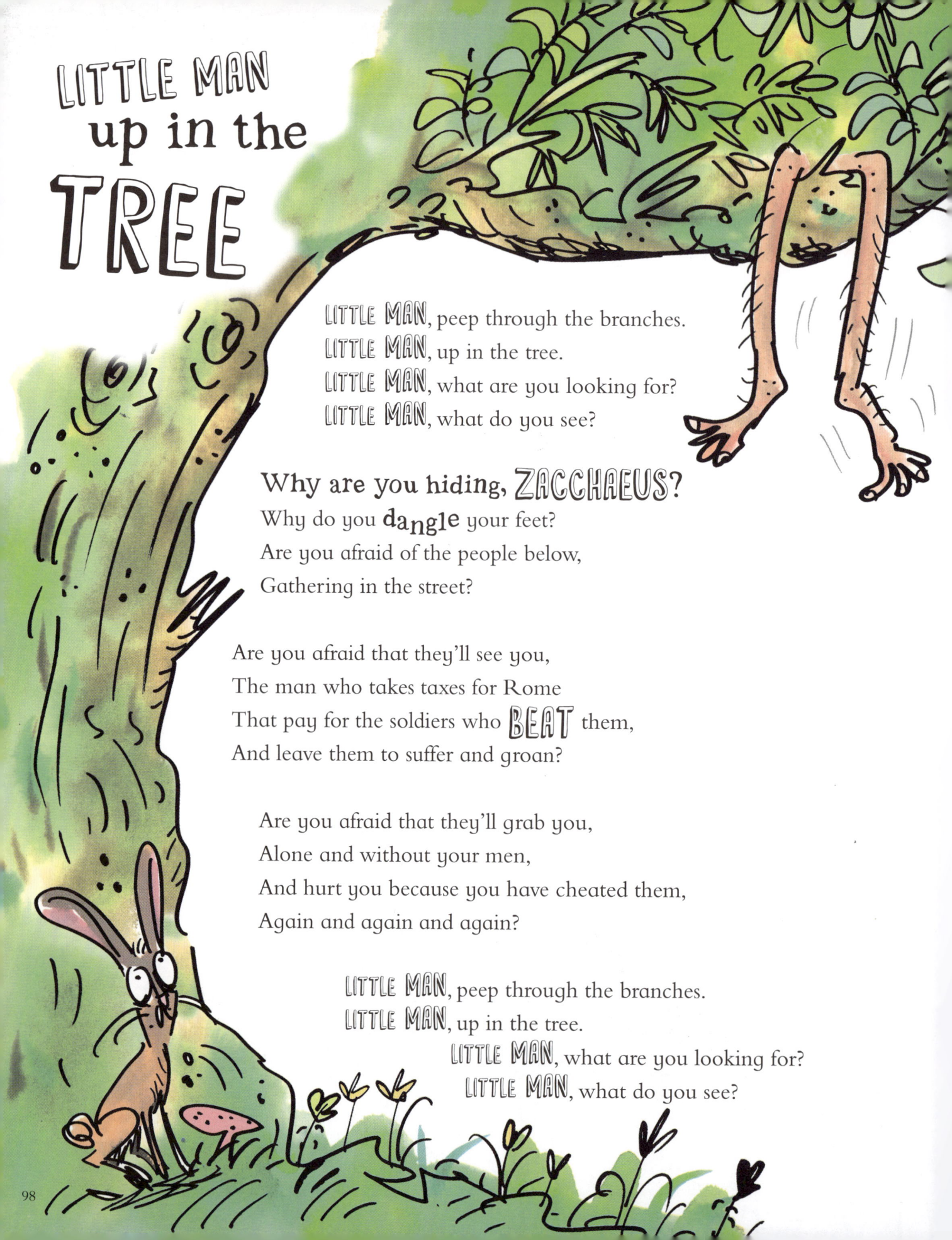

LITTLE MAN up in the TREE

LITTLE MAN, peep through the branches.
LITTLE MAN, up in the tree.
LITTLE MAN, what are you looking for?
LITTLE MAN, what do you see?

Why are you hiding, ZACCHAEUS?
Why do you dangle your feet?
Are you afraid of the people below,
Gathering in the street?

Are you afraid that they'll see you,
The man who takes taxes for Rome
That pay for the soldiers who BEAT them,
And leave them to suffer and groan?

Are you afraid that they'll grab you,
Alone and without your men,
And hurt you because you have cheated them,
Again and again and again?

LITTLE MAN, peep through the branches.
LITTLE MAN, up in the tree.
LITTLE MAN, what are you looking for?
LITTLE MAN, what do you see?

Jesus is coming, ZACCHAEUS.

Coming to Jericho town.

And everyone wants to have tea with him.

See how they swarm around.

'Come eat with me!' they all beg him.

See how he tells them all, 'No.'

He's looking for something, Zacchaeus.

Where do you think he will go?

Jesus is coming, ZACCHAEUS.

Is that who you're looking for?

Why would he eat with someone like you,

Who steals from the working poor?

LITTLE MAN, peep through the branches.

LITTLE MAN, up in the tree.

LITTLE MAN, what are you looking for?

LITTLE MAN, what do you see?

He's speaking to you, ZACCHAEUS!

He's spotted you up in that tree.

Listen, he's saying, 'Zacchaeus, come down.

Let's go to your house for tea.'

The crowd is now SHOUTING, ZACCHAEUS.

'Why would you go with that cheat?

Why would you spend time with sinners, Jesus?

Why would you go there to eat?'

Down from the tree now, ZACCHAEUS,
Off to serve Jesus his tea.
What will he say and what will he do?
It's all a big mystery.

LITTLE MAN, peep through the branches.
LITTLE MAN, up in the tree.
LITTLE MAN, what are you looking for?
LITTLE MAN, what do you see?

What's that you're saying, ZACCHAEUS?
You're sorry for being a crook?
You'll pay back the money you've stolen?
Four times the money you took?

You're helping the poor, too, ZACCHAEUS?
Everyone's shocked by your plans.
And Jesus says, grinning from ear to ear,
'Salvation has come to this man!'

Everyone's smiling, ZACCHAEUS.
And it seems that you're smiling too.
You thought you were looking for Jesus,
But Jesus was looking for you!

THE CLIP-CLOP BEAT

To the **CLIP-CLOP BEAT** of the donkey's feet,
Everybody *sing* your praises to the King.
As the people **SHOUT** and the stones **CRY OUT**,
Everybody *sing* your praises to the King.
Everybody *sing* your praises to the King.

Go into the village, said Jesus to his friends,
And find a colt that's never had a rider.
And if the owner asks, just explain the colt's for me
And that's the only reason you've untied her.

To the **CLIP-CLOP BEAT** of the donkey's feet,
Everybody *sing* your praises to the King.
As the people **SHOUT** and the stones **CRY OUT**,
Everybody *sing* your praises to the King.
Everybody *sing* your praises to the King.

So they went into the village and found the donkey colt
And led it back to Jesus like he told them.
They took their coats and put them like a saddle on its back
And Jesus headed off towards Jerusalem.

To the CLIP-CLOP BEAT of the donkey's feet,
Everybody *sing* your praises to the King.
As the people SHOUT and the stones CRY OUT,
Everybody *sing* your praises to the King.
Everybody *sing* your praises to the King.

Some laid their coats before him like a carpet on the road
While others cut down palms along the way
And laid them on the road as well, to make a leafy lane.
Then voices raised as one began to say:

To the CLIP-CLOP BEAT of the donkey's feet,
Everybody *sing* your praises to the King.
As the people SHOUT and the stones CRY OUT,
Everybody *sing* your praises to the King.
Everybody *sing* your praises to the King.

'Blessèd is the one who comes to meet us in God's name.
Hosanna in the highest, sing his praise!
Who brings the promised kingdom of David to his own.
Sing and SHOUT our God has come to save!'

To the CLIP-CLOP BEAT of the donkey's feet,
Everybody *sing* your praises to the King.
As the people SHOUT and the stones CRY OUT,
Everybody *sing* your praises to the King.
Everybody *sing* your praises to the King.

But some religious leaders were not pleased with what they saw.
'Tell them to be quiet,' they complained.
'If all my friends were silenced,' said Jesus with a smile,
'The rocks would sing instead and praise God's name.'

To the CLIP-CLOP BEAT of the donkey's feet,
Everybody *sing* your praises to the King.
As the people SHOUT and the stones CRY OUT,
Everybody *sing* your praises to the King.
Everybody *sing* your praises to the King.

BODY and BLOOD and BREAD and WINE

Jesus' disciples approached him and asked,
'Where should we eat the Passover meal?'
So Jesus gave two of them one simple task.
'Find a man with a jar. Keep your eyes peeled.

'And when you have found the man with the jar,
Then follow him back to his master's place;
And when you explain what you've been sent for
The master will show you an upstairs space.'

BODY and BLOOD and BREAD and WINE,
Given for you, a love that's all mine.
BODY and BLOOD and BREAD and WINE,
A supper that lasts till the end of time.

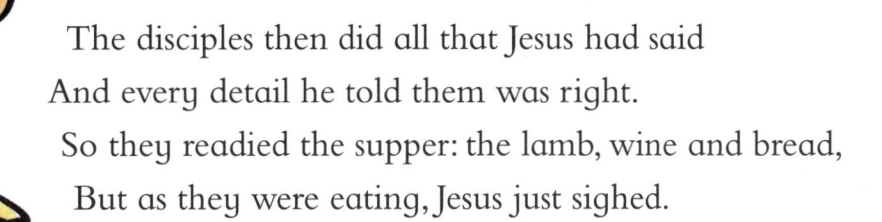

The disciples then did all that Jesus had said
And every detail he told them was right.
So they readied the supper: the lamb, wine and bread,
But as they were eating, Jesus just sighed.

'One of you here at this table tonight
Will betray me before we see a new day.'
The disciples all cried, 'IS IT I? IS IT I?'
'It's one of you, yes,' is all Jesus would say.

BODY and BLOOD and BREAD and WINE,
Given for you, a love that's all mine.
BODY and BLOOD and BREAD and WINE,
A supper that lasts till the end of time.

'One of you putting your hand in the dish,
Dipping your bread in this Passover stew.
I know I must die. I know that's God's wish.
But woe to the one who makes it come true.

'So listen to me,' he said, taking some bread.
And when he had blessed it, he broke it in two,
Then passed it to each of them. 'Take it,' he said.
'This is my body, given for you.'

BODY and BLOOD and BREAD and WINE,
Given for you, a love that's all mine.
BODY and BLOOD and BREAD and WINE,
A supper that lasts till the end of time.

He then took a cup, held it up in full view.
'Here is my blood,' he said, 'fruit of the vine.
The blood of the covenant, poured out for you.'
And when he had blessed it, they all drank the wine.

'Yes, this is my last cup of wine,' he said,
'Until, in God's kingdom, I drink it brand new.'
And when they had sung a hymn, he led them
Off to the hills, in the deep night's blue.

BODY and BLOOD and BREAD and WINE,
Given for you, a love that's all mine.
BODY and BLOOD and BREAD and WINE,
A supper that lasts till the end of time.

When JESUS hung upon the CROSS

When **JESUS** hung upon the **CROSS**,
His hands and feet **NAILED** to the wood,
He saw the men who hated him,
Laughing at him, where they stood.

Priests and rulers, one and all,
Some were jealous, some afraid.
'If you are God's son,' they mocked,
'Save yourself and leave this place!'

When **JESUS** hung upon the **CROSS**,
A crown of **THORNS** jammed on his head,
He saw the soldiers gambling for
What little clothing he had left.

He could have given hate for hate,
Or cursed the soldiers' hammer blows.
Instead he said, 'Father, forgive.
What they have done, they do not know.'

When **JESUS** hung upon the **CROSS**,
  He saw his mother's *tears flow down*.
    He watched her grief and agony,
      As she knelt weeping on the ground.

'John,' he called, 'disciple, friend,
Take my mother home with you.
Treat her like she's your mum now.
Do for her what I would do.'

When JESUS hung upon the CROSS,
Two **thieves** hung with him, left and right.
He heard one thief call, 'Save us now,
If you really are the CHRIST!'

'We're guilty,' said the other thief.
'This man does not deserve to die.'
'You'll be with me in paradise,'
Said Jesus to him, in reply.

When JESUS hung upon the CROSS,
His tongue HARD swollen, lips **cracked** dry,
He croaked, 'I thirst,' and then he saw
A sponge upon a branch raised high.

He wet his lips with sour wine,
And as he saw the darkness fall,
He cried, "IT'S FINISHED." Then he died,
For you and me, for one and all.

No more CRYING

When someone you love dies, you hurt deep inside.
You miss them so much you just want to cry.
The day Jesus died, his friends all hurt, too.
Peter and John and the rest of the crew
Were gutted and just didn't know what to do
With the **sighing**, GOODBYE-ING and *crying*.

Day one passed, then two, and on the third day,
Mary went early to visit the grave.
She went, with her friends, bearing spice and perfume
To anoint the dead body that lay in the tomb.
The day hadn't dawned, they walked in the gloom.
They were **sighing**, GOODBYE-ING and *crying*.

But when they arrived, they were filled with dismay.
The tomb had been opened, the stone rolled away.
So they went and told Peter, they went and told John,
'They've stolen his body, Jesus is gone!
They've moved him somewhere. Don't know what they've done!'
More **sighing**, GOODBYE-ING and *crying*.

So Peter ran off, but John, with a burst,
Sped right past his friend and reached the tomb first.
He didn't dare enter, just stuck his head in.
Only burial cloths, where Jesus had been.
'What's happened?' he wondered, his head in a spin,
Sighing, GOODBYE-ING and *crying*.

Then Peter arrived and, without delay,
Walked into the tomb, and where Jesus lay
Were neatly stacked sheets and the cloth from his head,
Like Jesus had woken and made up his bed.
Was it possible Jesus was no longer dead?
No more **sighing**, GOODBYE-ING and *crying*?

So Peter and John both went home, all amazed.
But Mary remained, and was suddenly dazed
When two angels appeared, shining bright, in the grave
At the foot and the head of where Jesus once lay.
'Where did they take him?' was all she could say,
Sighing, GOODBYE-ING and *crying*.

But before they could answer, she heard a voice speak.
'Why are you weeping? Whom do you seek?'
'It's the gardener,' she thought. So she quickly replied.
'It's Jesus,' she answered. 'Jesus who died.
If you've taken his body, please say where it lies!'
Sighing, GOODBYE-ING and *crying*.

'Mary,' he said, and, oh, what a surprise!
It was Jesus behind her!

JESUS! ALIVE!

'Teacher!' she gasped, but he told her to go.
'Tell all my friends what you've seen. They must know
That I'm no longer dead, I have risen, and so
No more **sighing**, GOODBYE-ING and *crying*.
No more **sighing**, GOODBYE-ING and *crying*!'

Not a GHOST STORY

Imagine that someone who died just appeared,
Someone you loved. Would it feel '**GOOD**' or '**weird**'?
So when Jesus appeared in a room that was locked,
His disciples were startled and frightened and **SHOCKED**.
'**It's his ghost!**' they all whispered, and every knee knocked,
Sighing, **GOODBYE-ING** and *crying*.

'There's no need to fear,' Jesus said with a smile.
'It's me, and I'm back. Well, at least for a while.
Touch my hands and my feet, you can't touch a ghost.
And ghosts never eat, but I'd like a fish roast.
My new body will last for for ever, no boast!
No more **sighing**, **GOODBYE-ING** and *crying*!'

But Thomas was missing and didn't believe
That Jesus had been, he still wanted to grieve.
'Unless I can see for myself', Thomas said,
'His hands and his side, the places he bled,
I won't be convinced that he rose from the dead.
I'll be **sighing**, **GOODBYE-ING** and *crying*.'

So Jesus returned to his friends the next week.
'Thomas,' he said, 'here's the proof that you seek.
Touch the holes in my hands, and the wound in my side.
See and believe that your friends have not lied.'
'My Lord and my God,' Thomas said, 'You're alive.'
And stopped **sighing**, **GOODBYE-ING** and *crying*.

For the next forty days, Jesus met with his friends.
Five hundred or so saw him living again.
Then he led them all up to a hilltop, on high,
And said, 'Let the world know that I am alive!'
Then up through the clouds he rose into the sky.
No more **sighing**, **GOODBYE-ING** and *crying*.

Blowing WIND and TONGUES of FLAME

Blowing wind and TONGUES *of flame*,
And then the Spirit came.
Blowing wind and TONGUES *of flame*,
And everything was changed!

Gathered in an upstairs room were
Jesus' friends, together.
But when the wind began to blow,
It wasn't just the weather!

God's Holy Spirit filled that place,
And TONGUES *of fire*, too,
Appeared on each disciple's head,
A sign of something new.

For TONGUES *of fire* soon turned into
Tongues of every nation.
And Jesus' friends could speak them all,
Without an education!

It was the feast of **PENTECOST**,
So Jews from every land
Were gathered in Jerusalem.
They didn't understand.

'These people are from Galilee
But somehow they can speak
To each of us in our own tongues,
In **Latin**, *French* and **GREEK**!'

But one man, not so courteous,
Said, 'This is what I think:
They're **babbling**. They make no sense.
They've had too much to drink!'

So Peter stood and told the crowd,
'These men are sober, friends.
God promised this, it's coming from
The Spirit that he sends.

'The prophet Joel told us plain
That one day we'd dream ***dreams***,
Men and women, old and young.
That day has come, it seems.

'For God's own Spirit falls on all,
The gift of JESUS CHRIST,
Who came to bring God's truth
And lead us all from dark to LIGHT.

'But right here in Jerusalem,
That man was crucified.
You killed the one that God had sent.
He suffered here and died.

'So God raised Jesus from the dead,
To live and never die,
And reign for ever on a throne,
Seated at God's side.'

Upset, the people cried to Peter,
'TELL US WHAT TO DO!'
'Repent and be baptized,' he said.
'Receive God's Spirit, too!'

So that is what the people did.
Three thousand were baptized,
And followed Jesus from that day
Reborn, renewed, ALIVE!

Blowing wind and TONGUES *of flame,*
And then the Spirit came.

Blowing wind and TONGUES *of flame,*
And EVERYTHING was changed!

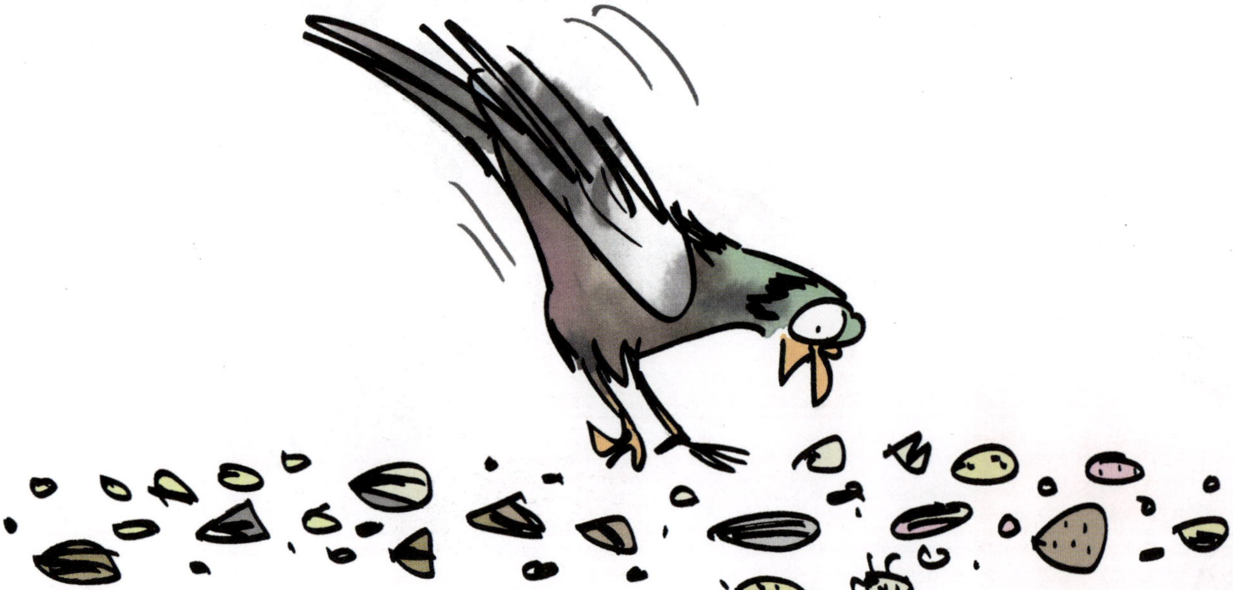